The Essential Workbook for
Algebra 2

A workbook for Essential Math Series

유하림(Harim Yoo) 지음

Preface

To. 학부모님과 학생들께

The Essential Workbook for Algebra 2의 출간에 앞서, 이전에 출간된 교재를 구매해주신 학부모님과 학생들에게 진심으로 감사의 말을 전하고자 합니다. 핵심 개념 교재들을 꾸준히 구매해주신 학부모님과 학생들 덕분에, 후속편으로 '문제풀이편'을 작업할 수 있는 원동력을 유지할 수 있었습니다. 이 교재는 Algebra 2 교과 개념편인 The Essential Guide to Algebra 2의 후속편이라고 볼 수 있는 교재로, 두 가지 측면을 생각하며 집필하였습니다.

첫째, 교과 과정 중 실제로 학교 시험에 나올 수 있는 내용 위주로 서술했습니다. 실제로 아이들이 써 내려가며, 자신이 놓치는 부분이 있는지 없는지 확인할 수 있도록 작성하였습니다. 문제풀이에서 학생들이 개념의 본질을 되새김질할 수 있도록 구성했습니다.

둘째, 경시 수학에 soft-landing 하길 바라는 마음으로 집필하였습니다. 한 문제 한 문제 Deep Thinking을 할 수 있도록 유도하였으며, 쉬운 문제라고 하더라도 깊은 생각이 가능한 문제 위주로 작성하였습니다. 이러한 내용을 기반으로 AMC10/12에서도 훌륭한 기본기로 잘 자리 잡길 바라는 마음이 가득합니다.

이 교재가 세상에 나올 수 있도록 지지해주신 피앤피북 대표님께 감사드리고, 이러한 교재가 나올 수 있도록 항상 지지해주시는 마스터프렙 권주근 대표님께도 감사의 마음 전합니다. 언제나 든든한 지원군인 제 아내와 딸, 부모님께도 항상 감사합니다. 마지막으로 제 삶에 많은 기회를 주신 하나님께 감사합니다. 앞으로도 더 좋은 교재를 만들어 견고하고 튼튼한 유하림 커리큘럼을 완성하겠습니다.

2024년 2월
유하림

저자 소개

유하림(Harim Yoo)

미국 Northwestern University,
B.A. in Mathematics and Economics
(노스웨스턴 대학교 수학과/경제학과 졸업)

마스터프렙 수학영역 대표강사
압구정 현장강의 ReachPrep 원장

[저 서]
몰입공부
The Essential Guide to Prealgebra
The Essential Guide to Algebra 1
The Essential Guide to Geometry
The Essential Guide to Algebra 2
The Essential Guide to Precalculus
The Essential Workbook for SAT Math Level 2
The Essential Guide to SAT Math Level 2
The Essential Guide to IGCSE : Addmath
The Essential Guide to Competition Math (Fundamentals)
The Essential Guide to Number Theory (Competition Math)
The Essential Guide to Counting and Probability (Competition Math)
The Essential Workbook for Geometry

이 책의 특징

유하림 커리큘럼 Essential Math Series의 개념 교재 학습 이후 공부하면 좋은 문제풀이편 교재입니다. 개념 공부가 한 번 끝난 학생들을 위한 교재로 적합하게 쓰이길 희망하며 집필하였습니다. 명문 Junior Boarding School 및 Boarding School을 진학하고, 교내에서 좋은 GPA를 유지하기에 필요한 내용들을 모두 포함하고자 힘썼으며, (8)9, 10학년에게 필요한 문제풀이 교재로, 현장강의 학생들에게 직접 적용하며, 피드백을 받아가며 작성한 교재입니다.

 ## 기본에 충실한 책

유하림 커리큘럼 Essential Math Series의 개념편에서 설명한 내용들을 토대로 작성하였으며, 학교에서 배우는 개념에 생각하는 과정을 입히기 위해 한문제 한문제 풀 때마다, 배운 개념을 떠올리고 복습하기 위해 좋은 문제들을 자체제작하여, 공부하는 학생들이 100% 이상의 효과를 낼 수 있도록 집필하였습니다.

 ## 생각의 확장을 위한 책

How보다 Why에 집중한 교재로, 왜 이 개념이 여기에서 적용되는지, 한 개념을 바라볼 때, 어떠한 마음가짐으로 봐야하는지, 개념의 본질에 집중하도록 제작한 문제들로 구성된 교재입니다. 말 그대로, 생각의 확장을 위한 교재로 교과 Algebra 2뿐 아니라, 경시 Algebra에서도 적용이 가능한 생각의 씨앗을 품기 위한 교재로 활용하길 바랍니다.

CONTENTS

Preface 2
저자 소개 3
이 책의 특징 4

Part 1 170 Problems 7
Part 2 Solution Manual 121

유하림 커리큘럼으로 Algebra 2 공부하는 방법
개념 학습 + 문제 풀이

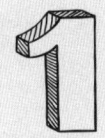 The Essential Guide to Algebra 2 개념 학습을 완성합니다.

 The Essential Workbook for Algebra 2 문제풀이를 답지를 보지 않은 상태로 풀어봅니다.

 The Essential Workbook for Algebra 2 답지에 나온 풀이와 자신의 풀이를 비교하며, 개념의 공백 부분을 채워넣고, 알고 있는 부분에는 확신을 가집니다.

저자 직강 인터넷 강의 : 유학 분야 No.1 마스터프렙(www.masterprep.net)

Part 1
170 Problems

Check-on Learning : Real Numbers

In Algebra 2, we mainly focus on the set of real numbers. There are some terms and vocabularies we should learn. Let's have a look at some basic terms.

- Opposite : This is also known as "additive inverse." Given a real number $x \in \mathbb{R}$, then $-x$ is an inverse of x. It is not difficult to see that the additive inverse of $-x$ is $-(-x) = x$.

- Reciprocal : This is known as "multiplicative inverse." Given a non-zero real number $x \in \mathbb{R}$, then x^{-1} is a multiplicative inverse of x. Like the previous term, it is not difficult to see that the multiplicative inverse of x^{-1} is $(x^{-1})^{-1} = x$.

Other than these terms, we have to look at some properties satisfied by the set of real numbers.

- Commutative Property : $x + y = y + x$ for real numbers x and y, and $xy = yx$ for real numbers x and y.

- Associative Property : $x + (y + z) = (x + y) + z$ for real numbers x, y, and z, and $x(yz) = (xy)z$ for real numbers x, y, and z.

- Distributive Property : $x(y + z) = xy + xz$ for real numbers x, y, and z.

- Identity Elements : 0 is called the additive identity, and 1 is called the multiplicative identity.

- Trichotomy : given two real numbers x and y, either $x = y$, $x < y$ or $x > y$. This naturally brings forth the casework when we see the condition related to "real numbers."

Another basic knowledge we should have known before tackling this question is 1) the definition of midpoint and 2) the distance between two real numbers.

1. The midpoint is the middle point of a line segment with given endpoints.

2. The distance between two real numbers x and y can be found by $|x - y|$ where $|x - y| = x - y$ where $x \geq y$ and $|x - y| = y - x$ where $x < y$.

where $|x|$ is the magnitude of a real number x that can be found by x (if $x \geq 0$) or $-x$ (if $x < 0$). As one can see, real numbers can be compared due to the property called "trichotomy." Not to mention real numbers, thanks to "Well-Ordering Principle,' one can list whole numbers from smallest to greatest, which is quite handy when solving some problems of ordering numbers.

001. True/False Questions

The set of real numbers satisfies the trichotomy property. Given a real value x, then we can think of three possible cases : $x > 0$, $x = 0$, and $x < 0$. This implies that two real numbers can always be compared in three possible cases. Solve the following problems, using trichotomy.

(a) If $x = y + 3$ for two real x and y, then is it true that $x > y$?

(b) If $x > y > 0$, then is it true that $\sqrt{x} > \sqrt{y}$?

(c) Given a real number $x \neq 0$, is it true that $x^2 > 0$?

(d) If $x > 0 > y$, is it always true that $x^2 > y^2$?

(e) If $|x - y| + |y - x| = 0$, is it true that $x = y$?

(f) If $|x - 1| = -1$ for real x, then there is no real value of x. Is this true?

002. Well-Ordering Principle

The Well-Ordering Principle states that we can always find the smallest element in a set of whole numbers or a subset of whole numbers. This can be proved by using the long-division algorithm and contradiction by assuming that there exists no smallest element in such set. Solve the following problems, using the well-ordering principle.

(a) If x is the smallest whole number, compute the sum of the three smallest integers greater than x.

(b) Compute the sum of the two smallest elements of the set of prime integers.

(c) Out of whole numbers whose remainder is 2 when divided by 3, compute the sum of the second smallest and third smallest numbers.

003. Difference of Real Numbers

(a) If $x = y + 2$ for two real x and y, then find the value of $|x - y|$.

(b) For some real numbers x and y, compute $||x - y| - |y - x||$.

(c) If $x > 0 > y$, compute $|x - |y - x| - y|$.

Comment

Given two real numbers x and y, we can always compare the two numbers using inequality. Either $x > y$, $x = y$ or $x < y$. Only one of the three inequalities holds true, which is also known as trichotomy. When we evaluate $|x - y|$, we first determine whether x is greater than y. If it is greater, then $|x - y| = x - y$. Otherwise, $|x - y| = y - x$.

004. Absolute-Valued Equation - Part 1.

If x is a real number, we use the inequality $|x| \geq 0$. If x is a non-zero real number, then $|x| > 0$, meaning that the distance from x to 0 is non-zero. On the other hand, if x is 0, then $|x| = 0$, meaning that the distance from x to 0 is 0. In other words, $x = 0$. This being written, solve the following absolute-valued equations.

(a) If $|x - 5| = 2$ for real x, find the product of all real solutions to the given equation.

(b) If $|x - 3| = 0$ for real value x, compute the exact value of x.

(c) If $||x| - 1| = 2$ for real value x, compute the number of real solutions.

005. Absolute-Valued Equation - Part 2.

(a) If $|2 - x| = 1$ for real x, find the sum of all real x-values satisfying the given equation.

(b) If $||x| - 3| = 1$ for real value x, find the product of all real values of x satisfying the given condition.

(c) If $||1 - x| - 1| = 3$ for real value x, find the number of all positive value(s) of x satisfying the given condition.

Comment

When there is an absolute-valued expression inside another one, we consider the innermost absolute-valued expression as a single expression, then use the casework in the last step, as stated in the solution to (c).

006. Basic Application of Inequality

Computing the number of integers described in the interval can easily be found by using one-to-one correspondence. For instance, a number of integers in $\{2, 4, 6, 8, 10\}$ has one-to-one correspondence with $\{1, 2, 3, 4, 5\}$. Here, we use the fact that dividing by a positive integer does not change the number of items in either list. In particular, adding/subtracting/multipling/dividing by some number to each number in some list does not change the number of items in the list. Hence, solve the following counting questions using 1-to-1 correspondence.

(a) Compute the number of integer n satisfying $11 \leq n \leq 200$.

(b) Compute the number of integer n satisfying $\sqrt{10} < n < \sqrt{111}$.

(c) Compute the value of integer n that implies 161 integer values of k satisfying $3^n < k < 3^{n+1}$.

007. Number of Terms between Endpoints

(a) Given an integer n, compute the number of integer value of ks satisfying

$$n - 2 \leq k \leq n + 5$$

(b) Given an integer m, compute the number of integer value of k's satisfying

$$m^2 < k < m^2 + 10$$

008. Number of Terms between Endpoints

As long as we can list the terms in the interval as a list of expressions from least to greatest, we can always use that information to solve math problems stated like below.

(a) If there are 100 integer values of k satisfying $n^2 < k \leq n^2 + 3n + 1$ where n is a positive integer, find the value of n.

(b) If there are 2002 integer values of k satisfying $n^3 < k < n^3 + 5n + 3$ where n is an integer, find the value of n.

Comment

Even if there are more than one variable in the interval notation, practice rewriting it in a list that we can count. For instance, if $n \leq k \leq n + 2$, for n and k integers, then $k \in \{n, n+1, n+2\}$.

009. Switching Integers into Radicals - Part 1.

Given a positive integer n, we can always write it as $n = \sqrt{n^2}$. This helps a lot, especially when we have to approximate a radical expression within an interval of unit length. Solve the following problems that use the fact $n = \sqrt{n^2}$ for positive n.

(a) Compute the number of integer values of n satisfying $1 \leq n^2 \leq 1024$.

(b) Compute the integer value of n that satisfies $\sqrt{900} < n < \sqrt{1000}$.

(c) Compute the number of integer values of n satisfying $41 < \sqrt{n} < 42$.

010. Switching Integers into Radicals - Part 2.

(a) Compute the number of integer values of k satisfying
$$\sqrt{k} < 2 < \sqrt{k+5}$$

(b) Compute the integer value of k satisfying
$$\sqrt{k} < 30 < \sqrt{k+2}$$

011. Deducing Midpoint Formula

According to the distance formula, given two real numbers x and y, the midpoint is located between x and y, and its value equals
$$\frac{x+y}{2}$$
However, one may use it in solving (a), but feel challenged about using it in (b). Try to deduce the midpoint formula to solve the following problems.

(a) Compute the midpoint between -14 and 16.

(b) Find the point on a real number line such that it is between 5 and 11 and the distance from 5 to the point is twice that from 11 to the point.

Comment

It oftentimes helps us solve inequality questions by plugging some values to see if they make sense. This is useful when we have no clue how to progress upon.

012. Conjunctive Inequality into Absolute-valued Inequality

There are two types of inequality we may see in Algebra 2.

- Conjunctive Inequality : "$a < x < b$," "$a \leq x < b$," "$a < x \leq b$" or "$a \leq x \leq b$."

- Disjunctive Inequality : "$x < a$ or $b < x$," "$x \leq a$ or $b < x$," "$x < a$ or $b \leq x$," or "$x \leq a$ or $b \leq x$."

(a) If $|x - 1| \leq 3$, then it can be written as $a \leq x \leq b$. Compute the sum of a and b.

(b) If $3 < x < 5$, then it can be written as $|x - a| < L$ where a and L are positive integers. Compute the value of $a + L$.

013. The Notion of Distance between Two Points

If there are layers of absolute-value inside an equation, make sure we casework every possible cases.

(a) If x is a real number satisfying $|x - 0| = 5$, compute the absolute-value of the product of all possible values of x.

(b) If $||x - 4| - |x - 2|| = 1$ for some real x, compute the sum of real solutions to the equation.

014. Casework

(a) If $|x - 2| = 2x + 5$ for real x, find the number of solution(s) to the equation.

(b) If $2|x - 1| + 3 = -2|x - 3|$ for real x, find the number of solution(s) to the equation.

015. Casework

If caseworking seems bit daunting, always start graphing from the innermost expression. Whenever we see the sign $|\cdot|$, we reflect the graph portion, which is below the x-axis, about the x-axis.

(a) If $|2 - x| = |5x|$ for real x, find the number of solution(s) to the equation.

(b) If $|||x| - 1| - 1| = \dfrac{1}{2}$ has n number of real solutions, compute the value of n.

Comment

Other than case-enumeration, we may use graphs to solve the absolute-valued equations. Here, we simply use the fact that the intersection point(s) of two graphs equal(s) the solution to the equations.

016. Approximating Radicals

Given $x = \sqrt{N}$, we can find the closest integer by looking at perfect squares near N. Likewise, if $x = \sqrt[3]{N}$, we can find the closest integer by looking at perfect cubes near N.

(a) Compute the integer closest to $\sqrt{1000}$.

(b) Compute the integer closest to $\sqrt[3]{730}$.

017. Radicals and Perfect Squares

Given a positive integer k, if we were to approximate $\sqrt{N}$ such that $k \leq \sqrt{N} < k+1$, we can find find the value of k by solving the system of equations

$$\begin{cases} k^2 < N \\ N < (k+1)^2 \end{cases}$$

Hence, compute the number of integer values of p satisfying $\sqrt{2} < p < \sqrt{1025}$.

Comment

Given a whole number n, we can always rewrite it as $n = \sqrt{n^2}$. In fact, the algebraic definition of $|n|$ equals $\sqrt{n^2}$. Thus, whenever there are radicals and integers intertwined inside an inequality, it is good practice to change an integer into radical expression whose radicand is a perfect square.

Check-on Learning : Coordinate Geometry

Given a set of ordered pairs (x, y) where $x, y \in \mathbb{R}$, we can plot the set of points on the Cartesian plane, where there are four quadrants, which can be identified by casework of the signs of x and y.

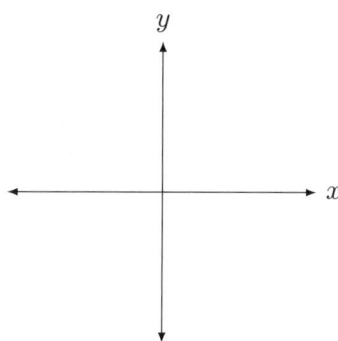

- $x > 0, y > 0$: the first quadrant.
- $x < 0, y > 0$: the second quadrant.
- $x < 0, y < 0$: the third quadrant.
- $x < 0, y < 0$: the fourth quadrant.

Additionally, coordinate geometry is extremely useful when we draw vertical lines or horizontal lines. In fact, the distance formula uses Pythagorean theorem with vertical and horizontal components. Given two distinct points (x_1, y_1) and (x_2, y_2), the distance between the two points is defined as the length of the segment connecting the two points, which can be computed as
$$d = \sqrt{(x_2 - x_1)^2 + (y_2 - y_1)^2}$$

The key idea is to break down horizontal and vertical components when we solve math problems related to the rectangular(= Cartesian) coordinate system. This implies that drawing horizontal or vertical lines passing through a given point will help us solve distance or area problems, using rectangles or right triangles. Likewise, we may utilize midpoint formula or interior point formula on individual axes, respectively.

018. Two-Dimensional Distance Formula / Pythagoras Theorem

If the one of the coordinates is fixed, try to find the distance between two points as the difference of the different coordinates. Otherwise, use the usual distance formula. Solve the following problems by using distance formula.

(a) Let d_1 be the distance between the points $(2000, 1000)$ and $(2000, 1001)$. Compute d_1.

(b) Let d_2 be the distance between the points $(5, 8)$ and $(2, 5)$. Compute d_2^2.

019. Application of Auxiliary Lines - Part 1.

(a) Let X be the area of triangle whose vertices are given by $R(0, 3)$, $S(1, 1)$ and $T(3, 2)$. Then $X = \dfrac{m}{n}$ where m and n are relatively prime integers. Compute $m + n$.

(b) Find the area of the triangle whose vertices are given by $A(4, 1)$, $B(1, 3)$, and $C(2, 5)$.

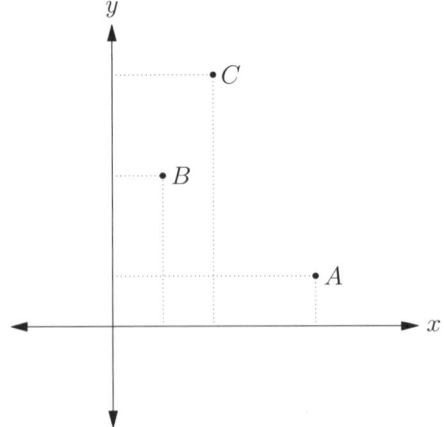

Comment

Other than the fact that drawing auxiliary lines passing through the given coordinates helps us understand why we use coordinate geometry, we may have to use useful information we learned in Algebra 1, especially slope information.

020. Application of Auxiliary Lines - Part 2.

The x-coordinates of points in coordinate plane have 1-to-1 correspondence to a number on a horizontal real number line known as the x-axis, and the y-coordinates of points in coordinate plane have 1-to-1 correspondence to a number on a vertical real number line.

(a) If the midpoint of a line segment connecting $P(2, 10)$ and $Q(6, -8)$ can be written as (m, n), compute $m + n$.

(b) If a point $(\sqrt{3}, 1)$ is rotated $90°$ counter-clockwise about the origin, then the resulting point can be written as (a, b). Compute $\dfrac{b^2}{a^2}$.

021. Application of Auxiliary Lines - Part 2.

If there is a point X between $P(2, 10)$ and $Q(6, -8)$ such that $PX : XQ = 2 : 3$, let (m, n) be the coordinates of X. Then, $m + n = \dfrac{p}{q}$, where p and q are relatively prime integers. Compute $p + q$.

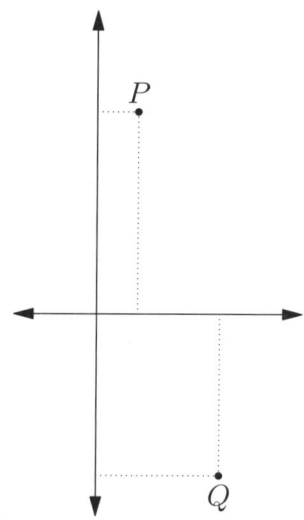

Comment

When there is a length ratio given, practice writing in terms of algebraic expression with respect to either x-coordinates or y-coordinates at a time.

022. Application of Distance Formula

(a) If A and B are points on the x-axis that are 7 units from the point $(3, 6)$, let $(a, 0)$ and $(b, 0)$ be the coordinates of A and B, respectively. Compute $a + b$.

(b) If two vertices of an equilateral triangle are $(0, 4)$ and $(0, 0)$, then there are two possible points for the third vertex of the triangle. Let $A(x, y)$ and $B(m, n)$ be the two possible points. Compute the value of $x + y + m + n$.

Comment

The word "equidistant" calls for application of perpendicular bisector. In fact, any point on the perpendicular bisector always forms an isosceles triangle with the endpoints of the segment that is perpendicularly bisected.

023. Analysis of Point-Substitution

Given a point (x', y') and a standard line equation $Ax + By + C = 0$, the distance between the point and the line is defined the shortest path from the point to the line, which can be computed as

$$d = \frac{|Ax' + By' + C|}{\sqrt{A^2 + B^2}}$$

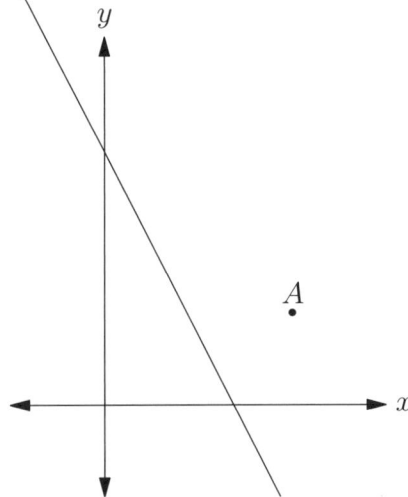

Let d be the distance between $(4, 2)$ and the line $4x + 2y = 11$. Then, $d = \dfrac{a\sqrt{b}}{c}$ where a, b, and c are positive integers, and b is square-free. Compute the sum $a + b + c$.

024. Application of Intercept-Form

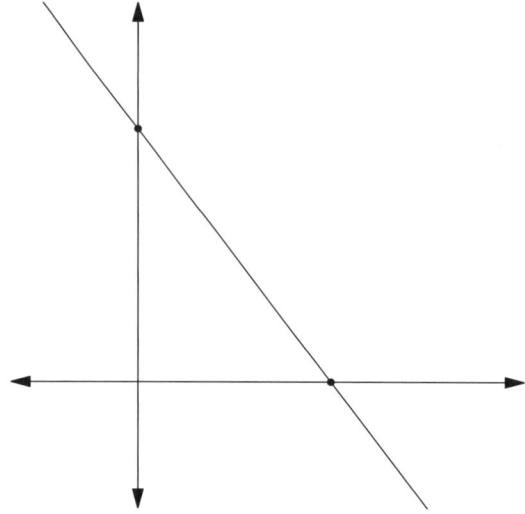

The graph of $4x + 3y = 12$ is shown above.

(a) Compute the area enclosed by its graph, x-axis, and y-axis.

(b) Let (m, n) be the point on the graph of $4x + 3y = 12$ such that the line passing through the origin and (m, n) is perpendicular to the original graph. Then, $m + n$ can be written as $\dfrac{p}{q}$ where p and q are relatively prime integers. Compute $p + q$.

Comment

When we figure out the x-intercept, we set $y = 0$. Likewise, we set $x = 0$ to find out the y-intercept.

025. Definition of Intercepts

Given $A(x,y)$, $B(r,s)$ and $C(p,q)$, the centroid is located at

$$\left(\frac{x+r+p}{3}, \frac{y+s+q}{3}\right)$$

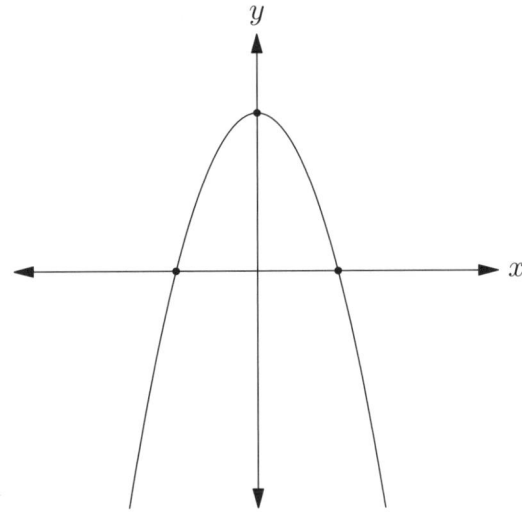

The graph of $y = 64 - 16x^2$ is shown above.

(a) Let P be the product of x-intercept(s) and y-intercept of the graph of $y = 64 - 16x^2$. Compute $|P|$.

(b) Let (m,n) be the centroid of a triangle formed by the x-intercept(s) and y-intercept. Then, the sum of m and n can be written as $\dfrac{p}{q}$ where p and q are relatively prime integers. Compute $p+q$.

026. Point/Line Symmetry - Part 1.

If a point is symmetric about the x-axis, then the original point and its image has their midpoint on the x-axis. Likewise, if a point is symmetric about the y-axis, then the original point and its image has their midpoint on the y-axis. Lastly, if a point is symmetric about the origin, then the original point and its image has their midpoint on the origin.

(a) Suppose a graph is symmetric with respect to the x-axis and $(1, 5)$ is on the graph. Let $A(x, y)$ be the point that must also be on the graph. Compute the value of $|x + y|$.

(b) Suppose that a graph is symmetric with respect to a point $(2, 7)$, and $(1, 5)$ is on the graph, as shown below. Let $B(x, y)$ be the point that must also be on the graph. Compute the value of xy.

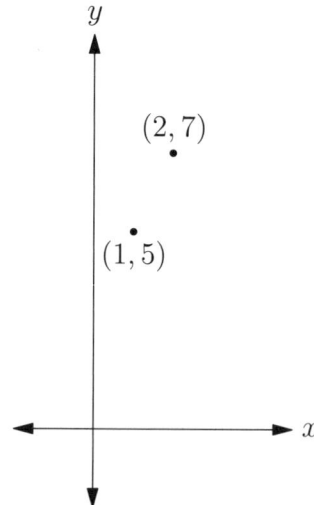

Comment

✓ If (a, b) is reflected about the x-axis, then the image must be $(a, -b)$.

✓ If (a, b) is reflected about the y-axis, then the image must be $(-a, b)$.

✓ If (a, b) is reflected about the origin, then the image must be $(-a, -b)$.

027. Point/Line Symmetry - Part 2.

If the image of reflection of (x_1, y_1) about the line $y = mx + b$ can be written as (x_2, y_2), then

✓ $\left(\dfrac{x_1 + x_2}{2}, \dfrac{y_1 + y_2}{2} \right)$ is on the graph of $y = mx + b$.

✓ $\dfrac{y_2 - y_1}{x_2 - x_1} \times m = -1$

That being written, as shown below, if $(1, 5)$ and (a, b) are symmetric about the line $y = \dfrac{1}{2}x$, then $a + b = \dfrac{m}{n}$ where m and n are relatively prime. Compute $m + n$.

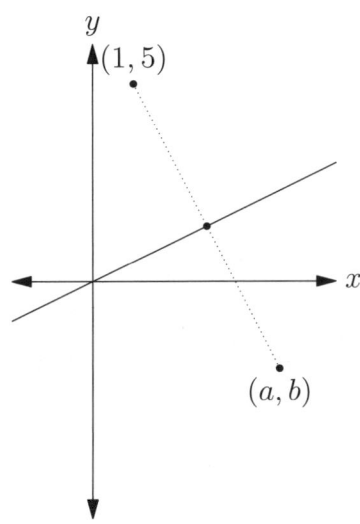

028. Point/Line Symmetry - Part 3.

Let $y = \dfrac{3x^2}{4 + |x|}$ be a graph. If $(2, 2)$ is on its graph, then there exists other point $A(x, 2)$ such that it has the same y-coordinate, satisfying $x \neq 2$. Compute the value of x^2.

029. Quadrants - Part 1.

If (x, y) is in the 2nd Quadrant, then $\left(-|-x|, |y|^2\right)$ is located in the nth quadrant. Determine the value of n.

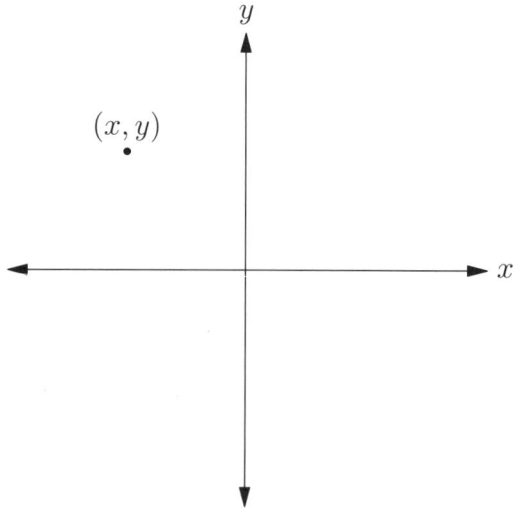

Comment

We normally call $f(x)$ an even function if $f(-x) = f(x)$ for all x in its domain. On the other hand, if $f(-x) = -f(x)$ for all x, then we call it as an odd function. Even functions have the graphs that look symmetric about the y-axis. Likewise, odd functions have the graphs that look symmetric about the origin.

030. Quadrants - Part 2.

There are two types of symmetries we find in either Algebra 2 or Precalculus. The first type is a line symmetry, whose graph consists of midpoints of the original point and the reflected point. The second type is a point symmetry, whose center of symmetry is the midpoint of the original point and the reflected point.

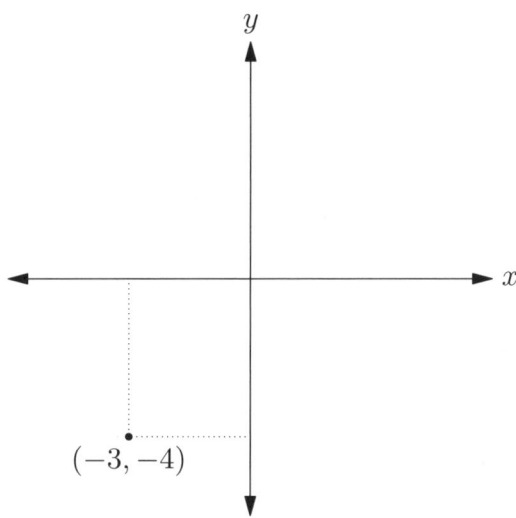

If $(-3, -4)$ is in the 3rd Quadrant, then the original point, the image of $(-3, -4)$ reflected about the x-axis, and the image of $(-3, -4)$ reflected about the origin make the vertices of a right triangle. Compute the area of right triangle.

031. Perpendicular Bisector

Given two points $A(x_1, y_1)$ and $B(x_2, y_2)$, the perpendicular bisector of $\overline{AB}$ is the set of points equidistant from either A or B. In fact, the perpendicular bisector consists of points (x, y) such that

$$\sqrt{(x-x_1)^2 + (y-y_1)^2} = \sqrt{(x-x_2)^2 + (y-y_2)^2}$$

If the perpendicular bisector of $(3, 7)$ and $(6, 4)$ can be written as $y = mx + b$, the sum $m + b$ can be written as an integer n. Compute the value of n.

Comment

Given two points A and B, the perpendicular bisector of $\overline{AB}$ can be found by

- ✓ using the distance formula.
- ✓ finding the line passing through the midpoint with the slope perpendicular to that of $\overline{AB}$.

032. Perpendicular/Parallel Lines

Given $y = mx + b$, then

- ✓ the line parallel to it has the slope of m.
- ✓ the line perpendicular to it has the slope of $-\dfrac{1}{m}$.

(a) If the graph of a line that passes through $(2, 3)$ and is perpendicular to the graph of $2x - 3y = 5$ can be written as $y = mx + b$, compute the value of $|mb|$.

(b) If the graph of a line that passes through $(1, 3)$ and is parallel to the graph of $3x - 5y = 1$ can be written as $ax - by = c$ for a and b are relatively prime positive integers, compute the value of $|c|$.

033. Intersection Point / Reflection

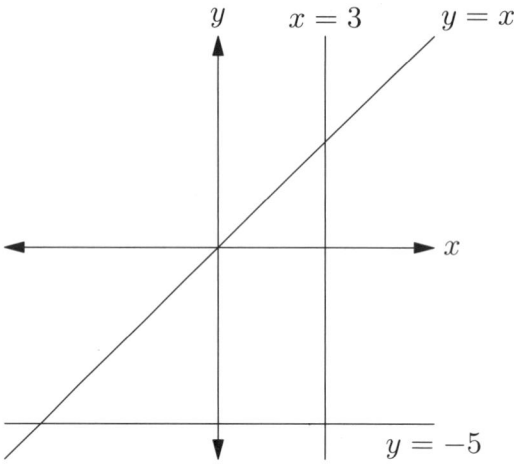

If the point of intersection between $x = 3$ and $y = -5$ is reflected about the line $y = x$, the resulting point can be written as (m, n). Compute $n - m$.

Comment

Given a point (a, b), if it is reflected about the line $y = x$, then the resulting point can be written as (b, a).

034. Parallel Lines / Reflection of Lines

(a) If the line equation that is parallel to $3x - y = 4$, containing the point $(2, 4)$ can be written as $Ax - By = C$, where A, B are relatively prime positive integers, compute C.

(b) If the line equation $2x + y = 4$ undergoes alternating reflections made about the x-axis and y-axis, then the resulting images form a bounded region that looks like a rhombus. Find the area of the rhombus.

Comment

The area of rhombus, given the lengths of diagonals d_1 and d_2, can easily be computed by
$$\frac{1}{2} d_1 d_2$$

035. Vertical Lines / Distance between a Point and a Line

(a) If the vertical line equation containing $(-5, -3)$ can be written as $x = m$, where m is an integer, let d be the distance from the origin to the line $x = m$. Compute the value of d.

(b) If there exists a circle that circumscribes a quadrilateral formed by four points - $(-5, -3)$, $(0, 0)$, $(0, -3)$ and $(-5, 0)$, then its circumdiameter has the length of $\sqrt{n}$ where n is a square-free integer. Compute the value of n.

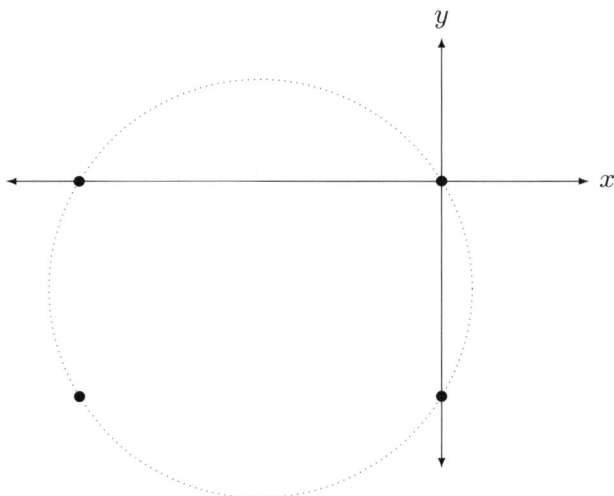

Comment

If a right triangle is circumscribed about a circle, its circumdiameter equals the length of hypotenuse.

036. Collinearity

The slope of a line never changes. In fact, this is well-connected to the application of ratio. In Algebra 1, we normally cover properties of collinear points as illustrated in the following ratio and the figure,

$$\frac{a}{b} = \frac{a+c}{b+d} = \frac{c}{d}$$

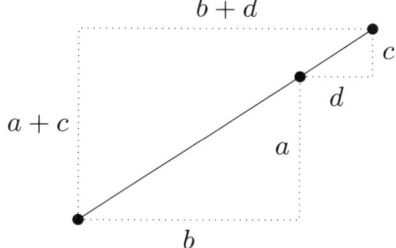

Hence, we can easily see that if three points are collinear, then the slope value for any pair of points is invariant. Use this information to solve for problems using collinearity. Hence, if the line equation containing $(3,4)$ and $(0,7)$ also passes through a point $(2a+1, 8)$, compute the value of $|a|$.

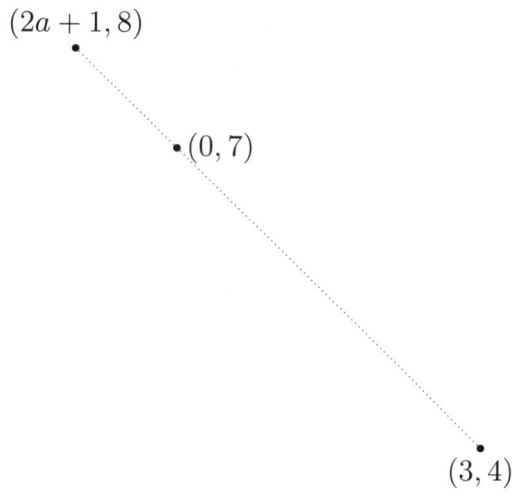

037. Distance between a Point and a Line

Given a right triangle, we can always find the height from the vertex of a right angle to the hypotenuse by using the area formula. In particular, if the base length equals the length of hypotenuse, then its height must be the length of the altitude from the vertex of a right angle to the hypotenuse.

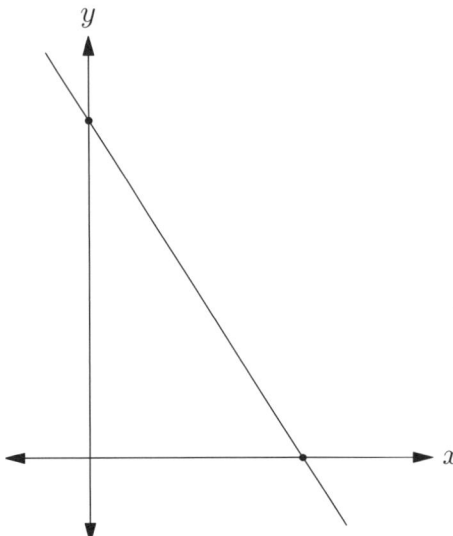

Let d be the distance from the origin to the graph of a line defined by $8x + 5y = 40$ as shown above. If $d^2 = \dfrac{p}{q}$, where p and q are relatively prime positive integers, compute $p + q$.

038. Distance between a Line and a Line

If two lines are similar, then we may have to use the fact about similarity. Let d be the distance between the graph of a line defined by $8x + 5y = 120$ and that of a line defined by $8x + 5y = 40$. If $d^2 = \dfrac{m}{n}$, where m and n are relatively prime positive integers, compute $m + n$.

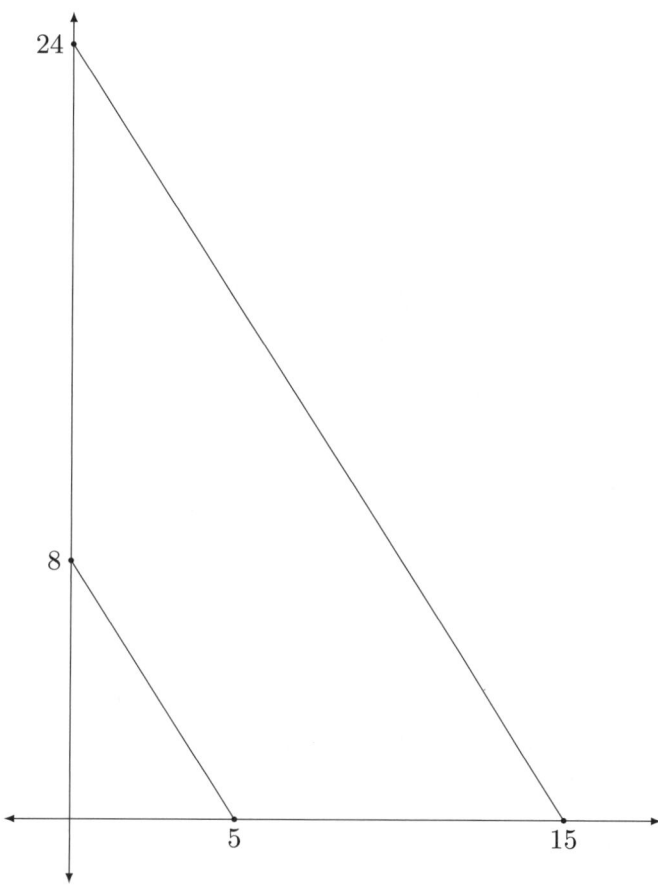

039. Parallel Lines

If the following two lines are equivalent,

$$\begin{cases} 4x + 2y = 5 \\ Ax + By = 20 \end{cases}$$

compute the product of A and B.

040. Perpendicular Lines / Number Theory

(a) If a line L_1 has a slope of $-\dfrac{4}{7}$, then the slope of a line that is perpendicular to L_1 can be written as $\dfrac{m}{n}$, where m and n are integers. If $90 < m + n < 100$, compute the exact value of $m + n$.

(b) Two lines, both passing through $(1, 2)$, have slopes whose sum is 3. If one line passes through $(4, y_1)$ and the other passes through $(4, y_2)$, find the sum $y_1 + y_2$.

Comment

Given some non-zero constants A, B, C, D, E, and F,

$$\begin{cases} Ax + By = C \\ Dx + Ey = F \end{cases}$$

✓ $\dfrac{A}{D} = \dfrac{B}{E} = \dfrac{C}{F}$ implies that the lines are equivalent.

✓ $\dfrac{A}{D} = \dfrac{B}{E} \neq \dfrac{C}{F}$ implies that the lines are parallel.

✓ $\dfrac{A}{D} \neq \dfrac{B}{E}$ implies that the lines intersect at one another. Specifically, if $AD + BE = 0$, then the two lines are perpendicular.

041. Function and Relation / Number Theory

From (a) to (d), if the answer to the following problem is "yes," then write it as 1. Otherwise, write it as 0.

(a) Is $(x, y) \in \{(2,3), (1,3), (4,3), (5,1)\}$ a function of x?
(b) Is $(x, y) \in \{(1,3), (2,3), (4,1), (1,5)\}$ a function of x?
(c) Is $(x, y) \in \{(1,1), (1,2), (1,3), (1,4)\}$ a function of x?
(d) Is $(x, y) \in \{(4,1), (3,1), (2,1), (1,1)\}$ a function of x?

Hence, write down the digits found in (a) through (d), from left to write. If the four-digit number formed by using answers from (a) to (d) is written in base-2, convert the number in base-10.

Comment

Given a base-n expression $\overline{abc}_n$, we may convert it into a counting number (which is another way of saying a base-10 number) by writing it as $a(n)^2 + b(n) + c$.

Check-on Learning : Linear Programming and Matrices

We delve into linear programming and matrices. The key idea of finding the optimal value in linear programming is to find the feasible region and compare values by plugging vertices of the feasible region in order to conclude maximal or minimal values.

Matrix is an array of numbers in rows and columns. For instance, given 3 rows and 2 columns, we can write one matrix as
$$\begin{bmatrix} x_{11} & x_{12} & x_{13} \\ x_{21} & x_{22} & x_{23} \end{bmatrix}$$

The following bullet-points teach us about the conditions of multiplication, the meaning of determinants, and simple algebra related to matrices.

- $A_{m \times n} \times B_{n \times p} = AB_{m \times p}$.

- Given a matrix $\begin{bmatrix} a & b \\ c & d \end{bmatrix}$, the determinant is $ad - bc$, where $ad - bc = 0$ means there is no inverse matrix.

- $\begin{bmatrix} a & b \\ c & d \end{bmatrix} \begin{bmatrix} x \\ y \end{bmatrix} = \begin{bmatrix} M \\ N \end{bmatrix}$ has no solution for x and y if $ad - bc = 0$.

- $\begin{bmatrix} a & b \\ c & d \end{bmatrix} \pm \begin{bmatrix} p & q \\ r & s \end{bmatrix} = \begin{bmatrix} a \pm p & b \pm q \\ c \pm r & d \pm s \end{bmatrix}$, adding/subtracting entries by entries.

- $\begin{bmatrix} 2 & 0 \\ 0 & 3 \end{bmatrix} \begin{bmatrix} p & q \\ r & s \end{bmatrix} = \begin{bmatrix} 2p & 2q \\ 3r & 3s \end{bmatrix}$. As one can see from this example, we choose to perform arithmetic operations on the rows of the second matrix.

- $\begin{bmatrix} 2 & 1 \\ 0 & 0 \end{bmatrix} \begin{bmatrix} p & q \\ r & s \end{bmatrix} = \begin{bmatrix} 2p+r & 2q+s \\ 0 & 0 \end{bmatrix}$. A linear combination of rows of the second matrix directly comes from matrix multiplications.

- $\begin{bmatrix} 0 & 1 \\ 1 & 0 \end{bmatrix} \begin{bmatrix} p & q \\ r & s \end{bmatrix} = \begin{bmatrix} r & s \\ p & q \end{bmatrix}$. Rows can be switched as well.

- The inverse matrix of $\begin{bmatrix} a & b \\ c & d \end{bmatrix}$ can be written as $\dfrac{1}{ad-bc} \begin{bmatrix} d & -b \\ -c & a \end{bmatrix}$, where $ad - bc$ is the determinant of the original matrix. The inverse matrix of A is denoted by A^{-1}, and $AA^{-1} = A^{-1}A = \begin{bmatrix} 1 & 0 \\ 0 & 1 \end{bmatrix}$.

042. Linear Programming - Part 1.

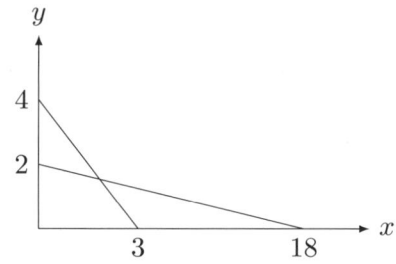

For real values of x and y, compute the maximum value of $3x + 2y$ if $4x + 3y \leq 12$, $x + 9y \leq 18$, $x \geq 0$ and $y \geq 0$.

043. Linear Programming - Part 2.

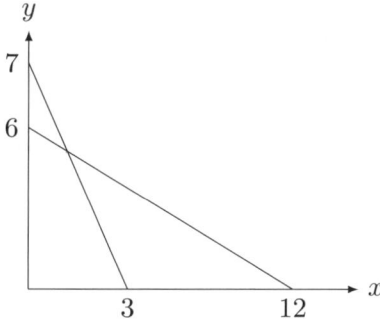

For real values of $x \geq 0$ and $y \geq 0$, if $2x + 4y \leq 24$ and $7x + 3y \leq 21$, the maximum value of $5x + 3y$ can be written as $\dfrac{m}{n}$ where m and n are relatively prime integers. Compute $m + n$.

044. Linear Programming - Part 3.

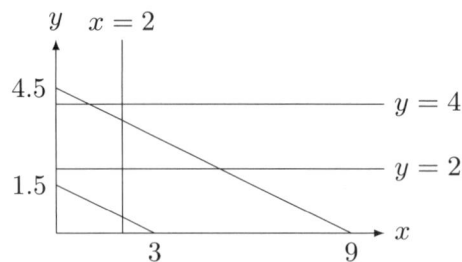

For real values of $0 \leq x \leq 2$ and $2 \leq y \leq 4$, if $3 \leq x + 2y \leq 9$, the maximum value of $5x + 3y$ can be written as $\dfrac{m}{n}$ where m and n are relatively prime integers. Compute $m + n$.

045. Linear Programming - Part 4.

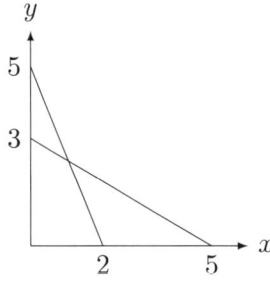

For real values of $x \geq 0$ and $y \geq 0$, compute the maximum value of $x + y$ if $3x + 5y \leq 15$ and $5x + 2y \geq 10$.

046. Linear Inequalities / Number Theory - Part 1.

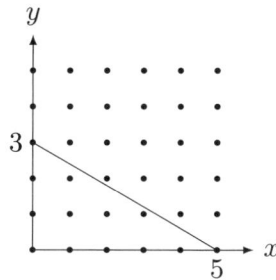

For integers x, y, if
$$\begin{cases} 3x + 5y \leq 15 \\ x \geq 0 \\ y \geq 0 \end{cases}$$
compute the number of solutions satisfying the inequality.

047. Linear Inequalities / Number Theory - Part 2.

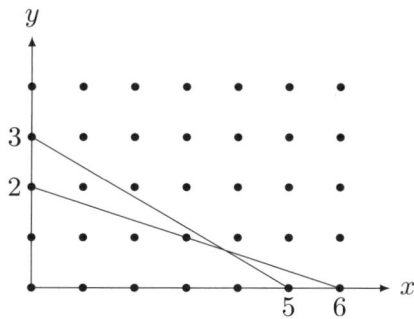

If $x \geq 0$, $y \geq 0$ for integers x and y, if
$$\begin{cases} 3x + 5y \leq 15 \\ 2x + 6y \leq 12 \end{cases}$$
compute the number of solutions satisfying the inequality.

048. Matrix Multiplication / Elementary Row-Operations

(a) Compute the sum of all entries of the following matrix product.

$$\begin{bmatrix} 1 & 0 \\ 0 & 1 \end{bmatrix} \begin{bmatrix} 0 & 1 \\ 0 & 1 \end{bmatrix} \begin{bmatrix} 0 & 1 \\ 1 & 0 \end{bmatrix} \begin{bmatrix} 1 & 0 \\ 1 & 0 \end{bmatrix} \begin{bmatrix} 4 & 3 \\ 2 & 1 \end{bmatrix}$$

(b) Compute the sum of all entries of the following matrix product.

$$\begin{bmatrix} 1 & 0 \\ 0 & 1 \end{bmatrix} \begin{bmatrix} 0 & 1 \\ 0 & 1 \end{bmatrix} \begin{bmatrix} 1 & 1 \\ 0 & 0 \end{bmatrix} \begin{bmatrix} 0 & 1 \\ 1 & 0 \end{bmatrix}$$

Comment

Elementary row-operations show a linear combination of rows in the right matrix. For instance, if $\begin{bmatrix} 2 & 0 \\ 0 & 1 \end{bmatrix} \begin{bmatrix} 1 & 2 \\ 3 & 4 \end{bmatrix}$, then $\begin{bmatrix} 2 & 0 \end{bmatrix}$ tells us to multiply 2 to the first row of the right matrix and do nothing for the second row. Likewise, $\begin{bmatrix} 0 & 1 \end{bmatrix}$ tells us to print the second row of the right matrix.

049. Matrix Multiplication / Elementary Row-Operations

(a) Compute the sum of all entries of the following matrix product.

$$\begin{bmatrix} 1 & -1 \\ -1 & 1 \end{bmatrix} \begin{bmatrix} 4 & 3 \\ 2 & 1 \end{bmatrix}$$

(b) Compute the sum of all entries of the inverse matrix of

$$\begin{bmatrix} 5 & 6 \\ 4 & 5 \end{bmatrix}$$

Comment

Given a matrix $\begin{bmatrix} a & b \\ c & d \end{bmatrix}$, its inverse matrix equals

$$\frac{1}{ad-bc} \begin{bmatrix} d & -b \\ -c & a \end{bmatrix}$$

050. Extending Elementary Row-Operations into 3 × 3 Matrices - Part 1.

(a) Compute the sum of all entries of the following matrix product.

$$\begin{bmatrix} 1 & 0 & 0 \\ 1 & 0 & 0 \\ 0 & -1 & 2 \end{bmatrix} \begin{bmatrix} 1 & 2 & 3 \\ 0 & 0 & 0 \\ -1 & -2 & -3 \end{bmatrix}$$

(b) Compute the sum of all entries of the following matrix product.

$$\begin{bmatrix} 0 & 1 & 0 \\ 1 & 0 & 0 \\ 0 & 0 & 1 \end{bmatrix} \begin{bmatrix} 1 & 2 & 3 \\ 0 & 0 & 0 \\ -3 & -2 & -1 \end{bmatrix}$$

Check-on Learning : Quadratics

Let's have a look at Viete's formula. If r and s are solutions to a quadratic equation $ax^2 + bx + c = 0$, then

- $r + s = -\dfrac{b}{a}$
- $rs = \dfrac{c}{a}$

Specifically,

$$\begin{aligned} a(x-r)(x-s) &= a(x^2 - (r+s)x + rs) \\ &= ax^2 - a(r+s)x + a(rs) \\ &= ax^2 + bx + c \end{aligned}$$

where $b = -a(r+s)$ and $c = a(rs)$, so $-\dfrac{b}{a} = r + s$ and $\dfrac{c}{a} = rs$.

That being written, suppose r and s are x-intercepts of $y = ax^2 + bx + c$, then

- The axis of symmetry $x = \dfrac{r+s}{2}$
- The axis of symmetry $x = -\dfrac{b}{2a}$

On the other hand, y-intercept is directly derived from the standard form of a quadratic function $y = ax^2 + bx + c$. It is simply c.

- x-intercept(s) : Set $y = 0$ to find the x-intercept(s).
- y-intercept : Set $x = 0$ to find the y-intercept.

Given $y = ax^2 + bx + c$, we can have a look at a. First off, $a \neq 0$ in order to maintain its quadratic property.

- $a > 0$: the graph is **concave up**, and it has a **minimum** value.
- $a < 0$: the graph is **concave down**, and it has a **maximum** value.

Now, let's have a look at discriminant, which tells us the number of *real solutions*. Given $y = ax^2 + bx + c$, we define $D = b^2 - 4ac$ such that

- $D > 0$: the graph intersects the x-axis at two distinct points : **2 distinct real solutions**.
- $D = 0$: the graph intersects the x-axis at one point : **1 real solution** (in fact, two repeated solutions).
- $D < 0$: the graph does not intersect the x-axis : **0 real solution** (but two complex solutions, by the Fundamental Theorem of Algebra).

051. Basic Factorization

Compute the positive difference of the solutions in the following quadratic equation by factorizing the following quadratics into a product of linear terms of x.

(a) $x^2 - 15x - 16 = 0$

(b) $x^2 - 24x + 143 = 0$

(c) $x^2 - 17x + 52 = 0$

(d) $x^2 - 12x - 28 = 0$

(e) $x^2 - 5x - 84 = 0$

Comment

According to Viete's Formula, we can always change $x^2 + ax + b = 0$ into $(x-r)(x-s) = 0$ form, which implies that $r + s = -a$ and $rs = b$.

052. Completing the Square

(a) Given that $3x^2 - 6x + 12 = a(x-p)^2 + q$ for all values of x, compute the sum of a, p, and q.

(b) If the equation of the quadratic function whose vertex is $(1,4)$ that passes through $(2,6)$, then its standard form can be written as $y = ax^2 + bx + c$. Compute $a + b + c$.

053. Vertex Form

Given $y = ax^2 + bx + c$ for real coefficients a, b, and c, if the y-value is equal for two distinct values of x, i.e., $x = m$ and $x = n$, then the axis of symmetry occurs at $x = \dfrac{m+n}{2}$. Hence, solve the following problems using this property.

(a) Given a quadratic function $f(x) = -6x^2 + 36x$ for all real x, compute the maximum value of $f(x)$.

(b) Given a quadratic function $y = 4x^2 - 16x$ and a line $y = m$, the number of intersection between the two graphs is at most 1. Let M be the maximum possible value of m. Compute $|M|$.

Comment

If $ax^2 + bx + c = a(x-h)^2 + k$, then $h = -\dfrac{b}{2a}$, whose value expresses the axis of symmetry.

054. Discriminant - Part 1.

Given $ax^2 + bx + c = 0$, we compute its discriminant as $b^2 - 4ac$, whose positivity/negativity implies the existence of real roots. Hence, solve the following problems using discriminant.

(a) If $x^2 + px + 2p = 0$ for integer p has rational solutions, then compute the number of distinct p-values.

(b) Compute the positive difference of p-values for which the x-axis is a tangent to the curve $y = x^2 + px + (p+3)$.

055. Quadratic Forms

(a) Let K be the minimum possible value of k such that the roots of the equation $x^2 - 2kx + k^2 = 3 + x$ are real. If $|K| = \dfrac{m}{n}$ where m and n are relatively prime, compute $m+n$.

(b) If the line $y = -x + p$ does not intersect the curve $y^2 = x + p$, the range of values of p can be written as an interval $(-\infty, P)$ where P is a rational number. Compute $\left|-\dfrac{1}{P}\right|$.

056. Quadratic Inequality

When we sketch a graph of $y = ax^2 + bx + c$ for $a \neq 0$, there might be some portion that is below the x-axis, which can be interpreted as $y = ax^2 + bx + c < 0$. On the other hand, there might be other portion that is above the x-axis, which can be interpreted as $y = ax^2 + bx + c > 0$. This being written, the solution set of each of the following quadratic inequalities can be written as an open interval (m, n). Compute the sum $m + n$ for each quadratic inequality.

(a) $x(x-3) < 4$

(b) $x^2 < 4x + 21$

Comment

✓ $a < x < b$ implies $(x-a)(x-b) < 0$.

✓ $x < a$ or $b < x$ implies $(x-a)(x-b) > 0$.

057. Application of Quadratics

(a) Given that $y = x^2 - px + 12$ and that $y < 0$ only when $3 < x < k$, compute the product of p and k.

(b) A line that passes through $(0, -1)$ meets the curve $x^2 - 4x + y^2 - 2y + 4 = 0$ at the point $(1, 1)$. If the sum of the coordinates of the second point of intersection between the line and the curve can be written as $\dfrac{m}{n}$ where m and n are relatively prime, compute $m + n$.

058. Circles - Part 1.

(a) If the standard form of the circle equation with radius 4 and center $(2, -3)$, can be written as $x^2 - Ax + y^2 + By = C$ for some positive integers A, B, and C, compute the sum of A, B, and C.

(b) If the graph of $(x - 3)^2 + (y + 4)^2 = 25$ intersects the x-axis at two distinct points, compute the sum of the x-intercepts.

Comment

Circle equation can easily be found by completing a square, as shown below.

$$x^2 - 2hx + h^2 + y^2 - 2kx + k^2 = r^2 \longleftrightarrow (x - h)^2 + (y - k)^2 = r^2$$

059. Circles - Part 2.

(a) If the radius of the circle equation $x^2 + y^2 - 6x + 8y + 11 = 0$ can be written as $\sqrt{n}$ where n is a square-free integer, compute the value of n.

(b) Find the difference of areas of a square inscribed inside the circle $x^2 + y^2 = 16$ and a square inscribing the circle.

060. Conjugates

If $3 - 2i$ is a solution for $x^2 + ax + b = 0$, where a and b are integers, compute the value of b.

061. Sum of Solutions

One root of the equation $x^3 - 3x + c = 0$ is $\sqrt{3}$. Determine the real value of c.

Comment

By Viete's formula, $x^2 - (r+s)x + (rs) = (x-r)(x-s)$. As it can be seen from the identity, we can deduce that the sum of roots equals -1 times the coefficient of x, whereas the product of roots equals the constant term.

062. Rationalizing Denominator

$\dfrac{1+i}{2-i}$ can be simplified into $\dfrac{a+bi}{c}$ where a, b, and c are integers. Compute the sum of a, b, and c.

063. Sum of Roots/Product of Roots

Suppose x is a solution to $x^2 + 1 = 10x$. Compute the sum of x and its reciprocal.

Comment

When we rationalize the denominator with complex number, always multiply by its conjugate. If we use some notations, for some complex numbers z and ω, then

$$\frac{z}{\omega} = \frac{z\overline{\omega}}{\omega\overline{\omega}}$$

064. Discriminant and Number Theory

The equation $x^2 - 4x + c = 0$ has imaginary roots. Find the smallest integer for c.

065. Application of Viete's Formula

Let a and b be the roots of $x^2 - 3x - 1 = 0$. Find the value of $a^4 + b^4$.

Comment

It is easy to check, by expansion, that $a^2 + 2ab + b^2 = (a+b)^2$. However, it can be transformed into $a^2 + b^2 = (a+b)^2 - 2ab$. This form strongly suggests that the sum of squares can be written as the sum of two numbers and the product of two numbers. In particular, if $a + b = X$ and $ab = Y$, then $a^2 + b^2 = X^2 - 2Y$.

066. Quadratic Inequality and Number Theory

Compute the sum of integer x satisfying $x^2 - 6x + 5 \leq 0$.

067. Transformation of Quadratic Graphs

If the graph of $y = x^2$ is reflected about the y-axis, translated 2 units left and 3 units up, the vertex of the resulting graph can be written as (m, n). Compute the sum of m and n.

Comment

When a quadratic function is transformed, always think it in terms of a vertex movement. It always helps us see how graph behaves in terms of a vertex. Given $y = ax^2 + bx + c$, if $a > 0$, then the left-side of the vertex must be decreasing, whereas the right-side of the vertex must be increasing. On the other hand, if $a < 0$, the graph increases then decreases from left to right.

068. Maximum and Minimum with or without Bounds

(a) Compute the minimum value of $y = x^2 - 6x - 1$ for all real x.

(b) The minimum value of $y = x^2 - 6x + 1$, given $|x| + |y| = 1$, can be written as $\frac{a-\sqrt{b}}{c}$ where a, b, and c are positive integers, and b is a square-free integer. Determine $a + b + c$.

Comment

If x is any real number, then $y = ax^2 + bx + c$ has its maximum or minimum at its vertex. However, if x is bounded below and above, make sure to see whether it contains the vertex. If not, then maximum or minimum might be located somewhere else.

Check-on Learning : Polynomials

For polynomials, here are some main vocabularies for revision.

- Multiplicity is either even or odd. If $(x-a)$ has **even** multiplicity, then the graph is **tangent** at $x=a$. Otherwise, the graph **cuts through** $x=a$.

- Degree is either even or odd. If the degree is **even**, the end-behavior is either **up-up** or **down-down**. Otherwise, the end-behavior is either **up-down** or **down-up**.

- y-intercept is the **constant term**.

The range of $f(x) = a_n x^n + a_{n-1} x^{n-1} + \cdots + a_0$ depends on the parity (even/oddness) of n.

- n is odd : the range is $\mathbb{R}$, the set of all real numbers.

- n is even : the range must be carefully computed by the graphic calculator, or calculus tools, which are beyond the scope of this book.

Also, remainder theorem and factor theorem, along with rational root theorem, are main topics covered in polynomials. Let's have a look at what they are.

$$\underbrace{P(x)}_{\text{Dividend}} = \underbrace{(x-a)}_{\text{Divisor}} \times \underbrace{Q(x)}_{\text{Quotient}} + \underbrace{P(a)}_{\text{Remainder}}$$

where $P(a) = r$, known as a remainder. This long-division algorithm of polynomial division is used for remainder theorem or factor theorem.

- **The remainder when $P(x)$ is divided by $x-a$ equals $P(a)$.**

- If $P(a) = 0$, then $x-a$ **must be a factor of** $P(x)$ because the remainder is 0.

Most of the problems in Algebra 2 assume that the coefficients are integers(or rational). In this case, by the Fundamental Theorem of Algebra, if a conjugate form $a+bi$ or $a+\sqrt{b}$ is given as a zero of polynomial, then the other conjugate form is automatically the zero as well.

- If $a \pm bi$ is a root of $p(x)=0$ for polynomial $p(x)$ with real coefficients, then $a \mp bi$ is also a root.

- If $a \pm \sqrt{b}$ is a root of $p(x)=0$ for polynomial $p(x)$ with rational coefficients, then $a \mp \sqrt{b}$ is also a root.

Lastly, there is a generalized version of Viete's formula. Typically, this formula is extended upto cubic polynomial equations. Let r, s, t be the zeros of $ax^3 + bx^2 + cx + d = 0$, then

- $-\dfrac{b}{a} = r+s+t$

- $\dfrac{c}{a} = rs+st+tr$

- $-\dfrac{d}{a} = rst$

069. Degrees of Polynomials - Part 1.

Determine the degree of the following polynomial functions.

(a) $f(x) = -x + 2$ (b) $g(x) = (x-1)(x+2)$ (c) $s(x) = x^3 - 4x^2 - x^3$

070. Degrees of Polynomials - Part 2.

x	1	2	3	4	5
y	4	7	16	31	53

The table above shows some values of $y = a_n x^n + a_{n-1} x^{n-1} + \cdots + a_1 x + a_0$. Compute the product of a_n and n.

Comment

When we compute the degree, we must simplify the given expression first. Now, the degree information can be used when we deal with table-values. In its last row of differences, the standard difference always appears as $n!$, given the degree of polynomial is n.

071. Cubic Functions - Part 1.

Determine the number of real solutions to $x^3 - 27 = 0$.

072. Cubic Functions - Part 2.

Determine the number of real solutions to $x^3 + 64 = 0$.

Comment

- ✓ $a^3 + b^3 = (a+b)(a^2 - ab + b^2)$
- ✓ $a^3 - b^3 = (a-b)(a^2 + ab + b^2)$

073. Integer Root Theorem - Part 1.

If r, s, and t are roots of a cubic equation $x^3 - 2x^2 - 11x + 12 = 0$, compute the sum $|r| + |s| + |t|$.

074. Integer Root Theorem - Part 2.

If r, s, and t are roots of a cubic equation $x^3 - 4x^2 - 31x + 70 = 0$, compute the sum $|r| + |s| + |t|$.

Comment

Given $x^3 + ax^2 + bx + c = 0$, then the integer root theorem states that possible integer roots are factors of c. This does not mean that the roots must be integers. It means that if there is an integer root, then it must be a divisor of c.

075. Integer Root Theorem - Part 3.

If k is a real root to a cubic equation $x^3 - 4x^2 + 5x - 6 = 0$, compute the value of k.

076. Rational Root Theorem - Part 1.

If r, s, and t are roots of the equation $2x^3 - 5x^2 - 14x + 8 = 0$, compute, the sum of positive real roots can be written as $\dfrac{m}{n}$, where m and n are relatively prime. Compute $m + n$.

Comment

Given $ax^3 + bx^2 + cx + d = 0$, then the rational root theorem states that possible rational roots are in the form of
$$x = \frac{\text{factors of } d}{\text{factors of } a}$$

077. Rational Root Theorem - Part 2.

If r, s, and t are roots of the equation $6x^3 + x^2 - 4x + 1 = 0$, the sum of positive real roots can be written as $\dfrac{m}{n}$, where m and n are relatively prime. Compute $m + n$.

078. Polynomial Inequality

Compute the integer value of n satisfying $n^2(n-2)(n-4) < 0$, whose associated polynomial graph is given below with the x-axis marked.

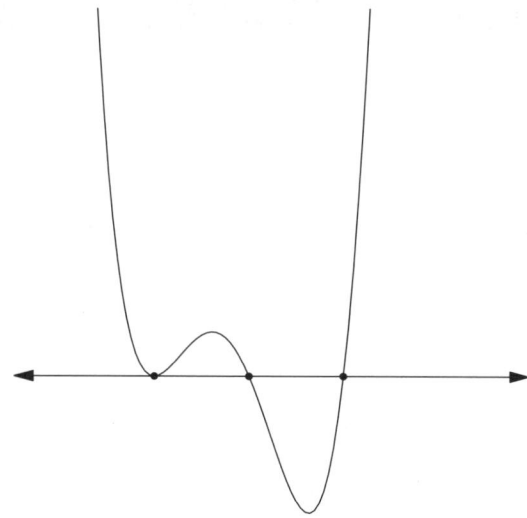

079. Remainder Theorem - Part 1.

Compute the remainder if $f(x) = x^3 + 5x + 4$ is divided by $x - 1$.

080. Remainder Theorem - Part 2.

Write all possible rational roots of $2x^3 - 10x^2 - 5x + 10 = 0$.

Comment

Given a polynomial of x, $P(x)$, if it is divided by $(x - a)$, then there exists some quotient $Q(x)$ with the remainder of $R(x)$, which can be written as

$$P(x) = (x - a)Q(x) + R(x)$$

081. Viete's Formula - Part 1.

If $f(x) = 2x^3 - 5x^2 + 10x - 1$, the sum of roots to the following equation

$$f(-x) = f(2x)$$

can be written as $\dfrac{m}{n}$ where m and n are relatively prime. Compute $m+n$.

082. Viete's Formula - Part 2.

If r, s, and t are solutions to $x^3 - 5x^2 + 3x - 1 = 0$, compute the following expression

$$(r+1)(s+1)(t+1)$$

083. Viete's Formula - Part 3.

If r, s, and t are solutions to $x^3 - 3x^2 + 5x + 1 = 0$, compute the following expression

$$|(r^2 - 1)(s^2 - 1)(t^2 - 1)|$$

084. Viete's Formula - Part 4.

If r, s, and t are solutions to $x^3 - 2x^2 + x + 1 = 0$, the following expression

$$(r^2 + 1)(s^2 + 1)(t^2 + 1)$$

can be written as n for natural number $n \in \mathbb{N}$. Compute the value of n.

085. Viete's Formula - Part 5.

If r, s, and t are solutions to $x^3 + x^2 - 2x + 3 = 0$, the following expression

$$\frac{1}{r} + \frac{1}{s} + \frac{1}{t}$$

can be written as $\frac{m}{n}$ where m and n are relatively prime integers. Compute $m + n$.

086. Viete's Formula - Part 6.

If r, s, and t are solutions to $x^3 + x^2 - 2x + 3 = 0$, compute the following expression

$$\left| \frac{1}{r-1} + \frac{1}{s-1} + \frac{1}{t-1} \right|$$

087. Another Application of Synthetic Division - Horizontal Translation

If $f(x) = x^4 + 5x^3 - 4x^2 - x + 1$, then $f(x-2) = ax^4 + bx^3 + cx^2 + dx + e$. Compute $|a| + |b| + |c| + |d| + |e|$.

088. Descarte's Rule of Signs

Assuming that $x^8 - 11x^6 + 41x^4 - 61x^2 + 30 = 0$ has no complex solution, compute the difference in the actual number of positive real roots and that of negative real roots.

Comment

The number of alternating signs of coefficients of $p(x)$ gives the possible number of positive real roots. On the other hand, the number of alternating signs of coefficients of $p(-x)$ gives the possible number of negative real roots.

Check-on Learning : Radicals

Given a radical expression $x^{\frac{m}{n}}$ where m is even number, for some relatively prime m and n, one must check whether x is real or not. Most of Algebra 2 math problems assume that x is real. Have a look at the following math problem to think deeply about radical expressions.

Let's think about the following expression.

$$x^{\frac{2}{3}} = 1$$

If x is real, then we ge $x^2 = 1^3$, so $x = -1$ or 1. But, what if x is complex number? $(-1)^{\frac{2}{3}}$ is not necessarily -1 because $(-1)^{\frac{1}{3}} = k$ for some k implies that $k^3 = -1$. This means that $(k+1)(k^2 - k + 1) = 0$, implying there are more solutions that $k = -1$.

Assuming that the inputs are real, the graphs of radical functions are different per index, which means that the domain and range of these functions are different per index.

- If the index is even, then the domain and range are the set of positive real numbers.

- If the index is odd, then the domain and range are the set of all real numbers.

Given a radical expression or equation, we should be able to

- rationalize the denominator.

- solve the radical equation.

The conjugate of $a + \sqrt{b}$ is $a - \sqrt{b}$. When we multiply the conjugate to rationalize the denominator, for instance,

$$\frac{1}{a + \sqrt{b}} = \frac{a - \sqrt{b}}{(a + \sqrt{b})(a - \sqrt{b})} = \frac{a - \sqrt{b}}{a^2 - b}$$

089. Simplifying Radical Expressions - Part 1.

If $\sqrt{(2\sqrt{2}-3)^2} = A + B\sqrt{C}$, where A, B, and C are integers, and C is a square-free integer, compute the sum $A + B + C$.

090. Simplifying Radical Expressions - Part 2.

$$\sqrt[10]{1024} + \sqrt[9]{512} + \sqrt[8]{256} + \sqrt[7]{128} + \sqrt[6]{64} + \sqrt[5]{32} + \sqrt[4]{16} + \sqrt[3]{8} + \sqrt{4}$$

can be expressed as an integer n. Compute the value of n.

091. Simplifying Radical Expressions - Part 3.

$$\sqrt[4]{16} - \sqrt[2]{4} + \sqrt{2}$$

can be expressed as an integer $\sqrt{n}$, where n is a square-free integer. Compute the value of n.

092. Simplifying Radical Expressions - Part 4.

For positive integer n, if

$$\sqrt{32} - \sqrt{8} + \sqrt{2} = \sqrt{n}$$

compute the value of n.

093. Radicals inside Radicals - Part 1.

If $\sqrt{3 - 2\sqrt{2}} = \sqrt{A} - \sqrt{B}$, for some positive integers A and B, compute $A + B$.

094. Radical inside Radicals - Part 2.

If $\sqrt{7 - 2\sqrt{12}} = m - \sqrt{n}$, for some positive integers m and n, compute $m + n$.

095. Rational Exponents - Part 1.

For real $x > 0$, if
$$2x^{\frac{4}{3}} + 1 = 17$$
then $x = a\sqrt[b]{c}$, for real x. Compute $a + b + c$.

096. Rational Exponents - Part 2.

For real $x > 0$, if
$$(x-1)^{\frac{2}{3}} = 4,$$
find the exact value of x.

097. Radical Equation - Part 1.

For real x, if
$$\sqrt{x+3} - \sqrt{x-2} = 1$$
compute the value of x.

098. Rational Exponents - Part 2.

For real x, if
$$\sqrt{x+8} + \sqrt{x+1} = 7$$
compute the value of x.

099. Radical Function - Part 1.

For positive integers $900 \leq n \leq 961$, compute the number of integers satisfying

$$61\sqrt{n} - 1830 > n - 900$$

100. Radical Function - Part 2.

Approximate the following radical number into the closest integer.

$$\sqrt[4000]{1,000,000}$$

101. Radical Expression

Given positive a, b, and c, if

$$\frac{\sqrt{a\sqrt{b\sqrt{c}}}}{\sqrt{c\sqrt{b\sqrt{a}}}} = a^x b^y c^z$$

then $|x| + |y| + |z|$ can be written as $\dfrac{m}{n}$ where m and n are relatively prime integers. Compute $m + n$.

102. Nested Radicals

Given an integer n, if

$$\sqrt{2 + \sqrt{2 + \sqrt{2 + \sqrt{2 + \sqrt{\cdots}}}}} = n$$

Compute the value of n.

103. Application of Radical Expressions - Part 1.

The width of a square is $x + 3$ and the length is $\sqrt{1 - 3x}$. Compute the value of $|x|$.

104. Application of Radical Expressions - Part 2.

The lengths of the legs of a right isosceles triangle are $x - 1$ and $\sqrt{7 - x}$. Compute the area of the right isosceles triangle.

Check-on Learning : Rationals

Typically, when a rational function is given, we are given with

$$f(x) = \underbrace{\frac{p(x)}{q(x)}}_{\text{Original}} = \underbrace{\frac{r(x)}{t(x)}}_{\text{Simplified}}$$

We may find about the domain, vertical asymptotes or holes.

- All values of x such that $q(x) = 0$ are undefined.
- If we simplify, the zeros of the canceled term(s) are holes.
- The zeros of $t(x)$ are vertical asymptotes.

Algebra 2 teaches us about the undefined value(s) of y. In this case, such undefined value(s) of y are known as horizontal asymptote(s). In order to solve it algebraically, rewrite $y = f(x)$ into $x = g(y)$, and look at the denominators of $g(y)$. For instance,

$$y = \underbrace{\frac{x-2}{3+x}}_{f(x) \text{ part}} \implies y(3+x) = x - 2 \implies x(y-1) = -2 - 3y \implies x = \underbrace{-\frac{2+3y}{y-1}}_{g(y) \text{ part}}$$

where $y \neq 1$ in the last part.

That being written, we may be asked to graph rational functions. One may approach the questions with the following tools - signed area method, sign analysis, and reciprocal functions. For those who are unfamiliar with signed area method, here is a brief snapshot of what it is.

If we are interested in sketching the graph of $y = \dfrac{6}{x}$, then $xy = 6$ implies that $x \neq 0$ and $y \neq 0$. This means that we get vertical asymptote $x = 0$ and horizontal asymptote $y = 0$. Then, we can easily plot $(6,1)$, $(3,2)$, $(2,3)$, $(1,6)$, $(-6,-1)$, $(-3,-2)$, $(-2,-3)$, and $(-1,-6)$ to sketch its graph.

105. Rational Function - Part 1.

Given the graph of of $y = \dfrac{4}{x-1} + 2$, compute the product of the y-intercept and the x-intercept.

106. Rational Function - Part 2.

Given the graph of $y = \dfrac{4x-8}{x-1}$, we can easily spot some points on the graph whose coordinates are all integers. For instance, $(2,0)$ and $(0,8)$ are intercepts whose coordinates are integers. How many points on the graph of the rational function have their coordinates all integers?

107. Rational Function - Part 3.

(a) If the $y = \dfrac{4x - 1}{x - 3}$ has the horizontal asymptote at $y = k$, compute the value of k.

(b) If the $y = \dfrac{4x^2 - 1}{x - 3}$ has the oblique asymptote at $y = mx + b$, compute the value of $m + b$.

108. Rational Function - Part 4.

If $y = \dfrac{x^2 - 1}{x - 2}$, the minimum value of y for $x > 2$ can be written as $a + b\sqrt{c}$, where a, b, and c are integers such that c is square-free. Compute $a + b + c$.

109. Rational Function - Part 5.

If the $y = \dfrac{4x^2 - 9}{2x + 3}$ is undefined at $x = \dfrac{m}{n}$ where m and n are integers. Compute the smallest possible value of $|m + n|$.

110. Rational Inequality

If $\dfrac{x - 1}{(x - 2)(x + 2)} < 0$ for $x > 0$, the solution to the inequality can be written as an interval (a, b) where a and b are integers. Compute $a + b$.

111. Nested Fractions - Part 1.

For real value of x, if
$$\frac{1}{1 - \dfrac{1}{1 - \dfrac{1}{x+1}}} = -100$$
compute the value of x.

112. Nested Fractions - Part 2.

For real value of x, if
$$\frac{1}{2 - \dfrac{2}{2 - \dfrac{2}{x+2}}} = 2$$
compute the value of x.

Check-on Learning : Exponentials and Logarithms

There are three types of exponential equations covered in Algebra 2.

- The easiest form is when the bases are equal.
- The intermediate form is when the bases are different.
- The challenging form is when the exponential expression is in quadratic form.

Equalizing the base is the crucial technique to solve exponential equations. However, if this is not possible, we either put log or ln in front of the equation to solve for x. The following list shows the properties of exponential and logarithmic expressions.

- $a^x a^y = a^{x+y}$
- $a^x / a^y = a^{x-y}$
- $a^0 = 1$
- $a^1 = a$
- $a^{-1} = 1/a$
- $\log(xy) = \log(x) + \log(y)$
- $\log(x/y) = \log(x) - \log(y)$
- $\log(x^y) = y \log(x)$
- $\log(x) / \log(y) = \log_y(x)$
- $\log_x(x) = 1$
- $\log_x 1 = 0$
- $\log(0)$ does not exist.
- $\log(x) = \log_{10}(x)$
- $\ln(x) = \log_e(x)$

Both exponential function and logarithmic function are either strictly increasing or decreasing function. In fact, this is a type of 1-to-1 function.

- If $a > b$, then $f(a) > f(b)$: $y = b^x$ where $1 < b$, or $y = \log_b(x)$ for $1 < b$.
- If $a > b$, then $f(a) < f(b)$: $y = b^x$ where $0 < b < 1$, or $y = \log_b(x)$ for $0 < b < 1$.

113. Exponential Inequalities

For each inequality, find the largest possible value of x that satisfies the given inequalities.

(a) $8^{x-1} \leq 64$

(b) $\left(\dfrac{1}{3}\right)^{1-3x} \leq 3^5$

(c) $\left(\dfrac{2}{7}\right)^x \leq \left(\dfrac{7}{2}\right)^{6-3x}$

Comment

✓ For $b > 1$, $b^x > b^y$ implies $x > y$, indicating that $y = b^x$ is a strictly increasing function.

✓ For $1 > b > 0$, $b^x > b^y$ implies $x < y$, indicating that $y = b^x$ is a strictly decreasing function.

114. Exponential Quadratic Equations

Compute the sum of real roots of the following exponential equation.

$$9^x - 12 \cdot 3^x + 27 = 0$$

115. Exponential Quadratic Equations

Compute the real solution to the following exponential equation.

$$8 \cdot \left(\frac{1}{2}\right)^{2x} + 2 \cdot \left(\frac{1}{2}\right)^x - 1 = 0$$

116. Continuously Compound Interest Rate

In a state park, the rabbit population was estimated to be 2000 and increasing continuously at the rate of 4% per year. The expected rabbit population in 100 years can be written as $a \cdot e^b$, where a and b are integers. Compute $a + b$.

117. Basic Definition of Logarithm

Evaluate each logarithmic expression.

(a) $\log_4 16$

(b) $\log_3 243$

(c) $\log_{17} 289$

118. Approximation of Logarithm

Approximate the following logarithmic expression to the nearest integer.

$$\log(1500) + \log(1050) + \log(1005)$$

119. Logarithmic Equations - Part 1.

Solve the following logarithmic equations.

(a) $\log(x) + \log(x-7) = \log(30)$

(b) $\log(x-5) - \log(x-3) = \log\left(\dfrac{1}{3}\right)$

Comment

✓ For valid values of A and B, $\log(A) + \log(B) = \log(AB)$.

✓ For valid values of A and B, $\log(A) - \log(B) = \log(\frac{A}{B})$.

120. Logarithmic Expressions

Evaluate the following expressions in terms of integers.

(a) $\log_4(2^4) + \log_2(2^3)$

(b) $\log_3(243) - \log_3(9)$

(c) $\log_7\left(\dfrac{1}{49}\right) + \log_7(343)$

(d) $\log_5(125) + \log_5(625)$

> **Comment**
>
> ✓ $\log_{a^m} b^n = \dfrac{n}{m} \log_a(b)$.
>
> ✓ $\log_a(a) = 1$.
>
> ✓ $\log_a(1) = 0$.

121. Logarithmic Equations - Part 2.

If the equation $(\log_3 x)^2 + \log_3(x^2) = 3$ has solutions r and s, then the sum of r and s can be written as m/n, where m and n are relatively prime integers. Compute $m + n$.

122. Exponential Equations - Parting Shot

For real x, if
$$9^x + 6^x = 2 \cdot 4^x$$
compute the value of x.

Check-on Learning : Sequence and Series

First, an arithmetic sequence is simply a linear function where inputs are whole numbers. On the other hand, a geometric sequence is an exponential function where inputs are whole numbers. That being written, arithmetic sequence is a sequence of terms with common difference. On the other hand, geometric sequence is a sequence of terms with common ratio. Now, let's have a look at the closed formula, which tells us the exact value for any value of n, for arithmetic sequence.

$$a_n = a_1 + (n-1)d$$

- a_1 is the first term.
- d is the common difference.

Similarly, we have a formula for geometric sequence, i.e.,

$$b_n = b_1(r)^{n-1}$$

- b_1 is the first term.
- r is the common ratio.

Second, the arithmetic mean is at least the geometric mean. When there is an Algebra 2 problem concerning maximum and minimum, you'd better think of trivial inequality or AM-GM inequality. Most of the times, AM-GM problems will be provided in rational expressions.

Third, math problems involving difference sequences can be solved by finding consecutive differences until they remain constant. The number of layers will be the degree, and the leading coefficient will be determined by the magnitude of the last layer.

The sum of sequential terms is called series. The sum of arithmetic sequence is given by

$$S_n = \frac{n(a_1 + a_n)}{2}$$

where a_1 is the first term, a_n is the last term, and n is the total number of terms. On the other hand, the sum of geometric sequence is given by

$$S_n = \frac{a_1(1 - r^n)}{1 - r}$$

Specific to geometric series, the formula for infinite geometric series is given by

$$S = \frac{a_1}{1 - r}$$

When solving summation problems involving sigma notation, one must remember that the index begins from the first term. Given some summation problems beginning with numbers other than 1, one must presume that the summation begins from the first term and subtract the unwritten first few terms.

123. Arithmetic Sequence - Part 1.

In a theater, there are 15 seats in the first row. Each row has 3 more seats than the row ahead of it. There are 35 rows in the theater. Find the number of seats in the last row.

124. Arithmetic Sequence - Part 2.

For the arithmetic sequence $\{100, 97, 94, 91, ...\}$, find the 10th term of the sequence.

125. Arithmetic Sequence - Part 3.

(a) Compute the arithmetic mean of 5 and 9.

(b) Compute the arithmetic mean of 101, 102, 103, $\cdots$, 107, 108.

126. Arithmetic Sequence - Part 4.

Compute the arithmetic mean of 1, 2, 3, 4, $\cdots$, 99, 100, and 101.

Comment

✓ "Expected value" is known to be the arithmetic mean.

✓ If we let X as a discrete random variable, then the expected value of X, denoted as $E(X)$, is $E(X) = \sum x \cdot P(X = x)$.

127. Geometric Sequence - Part 1.

Given a geometric sequence, $\{2, 4, 8, 16, 32, \cdots\}$, compute the 8th term in the sequence.

128. Geometric Sequence - Part 2.

Given a geometric sequence such that the first term is 2 and the common ratio is $\sqrt{2}$, compute the 5th term.

Comment

✓ Arithmetic sequence has its parent function form from a linear function.

✓ Geometric sequence has its parent function form from an exponential function.

129. Geometric Mean

Find the difference between the arithmetic mean and geometric mean of 4 and 16.

130. AM-GM Inequality

For positive real x, the minimum value of $x^2 + \dfrac{1}{x^2}$ can be written as an integer n. Compute the value of n.

Comment

- ✓ For positive real x, y, then $\frac{x+y}{2} \geq \sqrt{xy}$.
- ✓ For positive real x, y, and z, then $\frac{x+y+z}{3} \geq \sqrt[3]{xyz}$.

131. Arithmetic Series

(a) Given an arithmetic sequence $a_n = 4n + 1$ for $n \in \mathbb{N}$, compute the sum of the first ten terms.

(b) Given an arithmetic sequence $a_n = 3n - 1$ for $n \in \mathbb{N}$, compute the sum of the first seven terms.

132. Geometric Series

(a) Given a geometric sequence $b_n = 2 \cdot \left(\dfrac{1}{2}\right)^{n-1}$, the sum of the first five terms can be written as $\dfrac{m}{n}$ where m and n are relatively prime integers. Compute $m + n$.

(b) Given a geometric sequence $c_n = 4 \cdot \left(-\dfrac{1}{2}\right)^{n-1}$, the sum of the infinitely many terms of the sequence can be written as $\dfrac{m}{n}$ where m and n are relatively prime integers. Compute $m + n$.

133. Sigma Notation - Part 1.

Evaluate the following series.
$$\sum_{k=1}^{20}(k+1)(k+2)$$

134. Sigma Notation - Part 2.

Evaluate the following series.
$$\sum_{k=1}^{7}(k+1)^3$$

135. Infinite Series mixed with Arithmetic and Geometric Series

Evaluate the following infinite series.

$$\frac{1}{2} + \frac{2}{2^2} + \frac{3}{2^3} + \frac{4}{2^4} + \cdots$$

136. Sequence and Series

For $n \in \mathbb{N}$,

$$S_n = \sum_{k=1}^{n} a_k = 4n^2 + 3n + 1$$

compute the value of a_{10}.

137. Difference Sequence - Part 1.

n	1	2	3	4	5
x_n	3	9	19	33	51

If $x_n = a_k n^k + a_{k-1} n^{k-1} + \cdots + a_0$, compute the product of a_k and k.

138. Difference Sequence - Part 2.

n	1	2	3	4	5	6
x_n	2	11	34	77	146	247

If $x_n = a_k n^k + a_{k-1} n^{k-1} + \cdots + a_0$, compute the sum of a_k and k.

139. Recursion - Part 1.

If Bob can walk by either 1-step or 2-steps, in how many ways can Bob go up 10 steps in total?

140. Recursion - Part 2.

If Bob can walk by either 1-step or 2-steps, in how many ways can Bob go up 10 steps in total, assuming that Bob cannot walk two consecutive 2-steps in a row?

Check-on Learning : Counting and Probability

First, according to fundamental theorem of counting, we either **add** or **multiply** when we count.

- If "A, then B", we (**multiply** / add).

- If "either A or B, we (multiply / **add**).

Specifically, here are the helpful queues for solving counting problems.

- We *multiply* when two events are **successive**.

- We also *multiply* if calculations are **repetitive**.

- We *add* when two events **do not happen** at the same time.

- We *add* if calculations are **different**.

According to the principle of inclusion and exclusion,

- $n(A \cup B) = n(A) + n(B) - n(A \cap B)$

- $n(A \cap B) = n(B) \times n(A|B)$

- $n(B|A) = n(B)$ if A and B are **independent**. Normally, the subject test assumes two events are independent.

- We *subtract* if events are **overcounted**.

That being written, probability is all about proportion. The probability of an event A is the ratio of the number of ways A can happen to the total number of outcomes. Computational mechanism follows both principles of addition and multiplication. If events A or B cannot occur at the same time, we simply add probabilities. On the other hand, if events A and B can happen *simultaneously* or *successively*, then we multiply the probabilities.

- If you see the phrase **at least**, perform **complementary counting**.

- If you see the phrase similar to **given that**, then the **sample space** shrinks, where sample space is the set of all possible outcomes.

Now, probability distribution function may fall under discrete random variable or continuous random variable. For discrete random variable, we may assign probability to each value of the variable such that the sum of the probability is 1, and none of the probability is negative nor greater than 1.

If a data set of continuous variable is normally distributed, then the following normal curve is drawn such that the highest peak is mean, median, and mode at the same time, which means that the graph is symmetric about the vertical line that passes through the mean value.

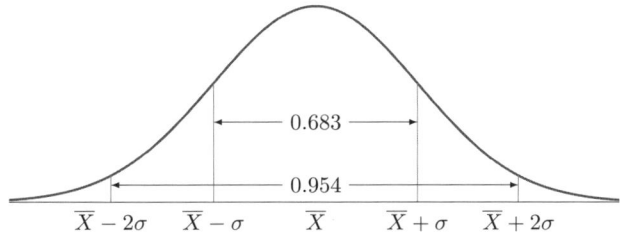

Normally, the data set does not have the mean value of 0, nor the standard deviation of 0. However, there is a technique called $Z-$ transformation that converts any specific normal distribution into the standard normal distribution with the mean of 0 and standard deviation of 1. $Z-$ transformation is specifically good for relative comparison between data values from different data sets with normal distributions.

$$Z - \text{score} = \frac{\text{data} - \text{mean}}{\text{standard deviation}}$$

Let's have a look at the graph of standard normal distribution curve.

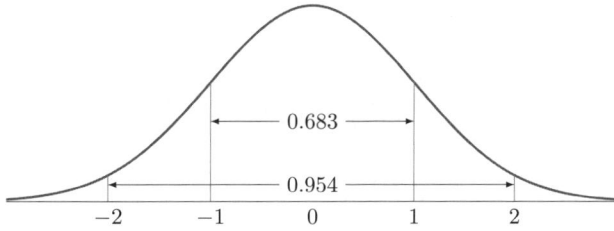

- $Z = 0$ is the line that is 0 standard deviation away from the mean.

- As shown in the figure above, the standard deviation shows an interesting property that approximately 68% of the values lie within one standard deviation from the mean and about 95% of the values like within two standard deviations from the mean. Within three standard deviations, nearly all portions of the graph can be fully explained.

- The area under the curve is equal to 1, and portions of the graph mean the probability that the data is included in that region.

141. Casework

When two different fair dice are thrown, compute the number of cases when the sum of the face values is a multiple of 3.

142. Principle of Inclusion and Exclusion

Compute the number of multiples of 5 or 7 for integers from 1 to 100.

143. Multiplication Principle of Counting - Part 1.

Compute the number of distinct terms in the expansion of

$$(x_1 + x_2)(y_1 + y_2 + y_3)(z_1 + z_2 + z_3 + z_4)$$

144. Multiplication Principle of Counting - Part 2.

If there are four paths from A to B, and five paths from B to C, find the total number of paths from A to C, assuming that the path must use the minimum number of paths, and it must go through B to reach C.

145. Permutation / Number of Divisors

A soccer association runs a tournament with 16 teams. If there are n different ways the top 8 positions can be filled in the end, assuming that no team can tie, then there are $f(n)$ number of positive divisors of n. Compute the value of $f(n)$.

146. Combination with Restrictions

Compute the number of different teams of 4 people that can be selected from a squad of 7 people, including Bob, if

(a) the team must include Bob;

(b) the team must exclude Bob.

147. Permutation with Restrictions

Given a set of natural numbers $\{1, 2, 3, \cdots, 7, 8\}$, if a four-digit number is formed whose sum of any two digits is not 9, compute the number of four-digit numbers satisfying the given condition.

148. Permutation with Restrictions / Casework

Suppose Alice and Bob are joining two clubs each from four different clubs. Compute the total number of ways for them to join the clubs such that the common club they join together is at most one.

149. Permutation with Restrictions / Casework

If there are 8 different cards whose face value is written from 1 to 8, suppose we "select" 5 different cards at the same time. Compute the number of ways that the sum of all face values of 5 cards is even.

150. Adjacency / Non-adjacency

If there are 2 different history books, 3 distinct novels, and 4 distinct comic books, compute the number of arrangements of these books such that no history book is adjacent to one another.

151. Adjacency / Non-adjacency

If there are 2 different history books, 2 distinct novels, and 3 distinct comic books, compute the number of arrangements of these books such that all comic books are adjacent to one another.

152. Circular Permutation - Part 1.

If six people are to be seated around a circular table, equidistant from one another, in how many ways can all the people be seated, assuming that two configurations are considered equal if one configuration can be rotated to be another one?

153. Circular Permutation - Part 2.

If seven people, including Bob and Bo, are to be seated around a circular table, equidistant from one another, in how many ways call all seven people be seated such that Bob and Bo are adjacent to one another, assuming that two configurations are considered equal if one configuration can be rotated to be another one?

154. Circular Permutation - Part 2.

If six people, including Alice and Bob, are to be seated around a circular table, equidistant from one another, in how many ways call all six people be seated such that Alice and Bob are NOT adjacent to one another, assuming that two configurations are considered equal if one configuration can be rotated to be another one?

155. Probability - Part 1.

An urn contains balls labeled from 1 to 5. If three balls are taken at a time and replaced again to the urn, the probability that an odd number is selected exactly once can be written as m/n where m and n are relatively prime. Compute $m + n$.

156. Probability - Part 2.

Let p be the probability that a prime is less than 10, given that it is less than 18. Then, $p = m/n$ where m and n are relatively prime integers. Compute $m + n$.

157. Probability - Part 3.

If the probability that Real Madrid will win the Champions League is 1/3 and if the probability that Chelsea will win FA Cup is 1/4, let p be the probability that only one of these teams will win its respective championship. If $p = m/n$ where m and n are relatively prime integers, compute $m + n$.

158. Probability - Part 4.

Out of seven people, three of whom are "biological" males, let p be the probability of selecting two people of different "biological" gender. If $p = m/n$, where m and n are relatively prime, compute $m + n$.

159. Probability - Part 5.

If two coins are removed at random from a box containing three nickels and eight dimes, let p be the probability that both coins will be nickels. If $p = m/n$, where m and n are relatively prime integers, compute $m + n$.

160. Probability - Part 6.

Seven blue marbles and six red marbles are held in a single container. Marbles are randomly selected one at a time and not returned to the container. If the first two marbles selected are both blue, let p be the probability that at least one red marble will be chosen in the next two selections. If $p = m/n$, where m and n are relatively prime integers, compute $m + n$.

161. Probability - Part 7.

If a single fair die is tossed, let p be the probability of obtaining either a multiple of 2 or 3. If $p = m/n$, where m and n are relatively prime positive integers, compute $m + n$.

162. Probability - Part 8.

If the probability of a certain team winning is always $\frac{3}{4}$, let p the probability that this team will win its first three matches and lose the last fourth match. If $p = m/n$, where m and n are relatively prime, compute $m + n$.

163. Probability - Part 9.

A coin is tossed four times. Given that at least one head appears, let p be the probability that exactly two heads appear. If $p = m/n$, where m and n are relatively prime integers, compute $m + n$.

164. Probability - Part 10.

A committee of 5 people is to be selected from 6 men and 9 women. If the selection is randomly made, let p be the probability that the committee consists of 3 men and 2 women. If $p = m/n$ where m and n are relatively prime, compute the sum of distinct prime factors of n.

165. Probability Distribution Function - Part 1.

Given the following probability distribution function,

x	1	2	3	4
$p(x)$	1/4	1/3	1/4	1/6

if the expected value (or mean) can be written as $\dfrac{m}{n}$ where m and n are relatively prime integers, compute $m + n$.

166. Probability Distribution Function - Part 2.

x	1	2	3	4
$p(x)$	1/4	1/4	1/4	1/4

compute the variance.

167. Probability Distribution Function - Part 3.

If a random variable $X \sim B(5, 0.2)$ can be modeled by the binomial distribution function, let p be the probability when there are three "successes" in the binomial distribution model. If $p = m/n$, where m and n are relatively prime, compute $m + n$.

168. Probability Distribution Function - Part 4.

If a random variable $X \sim N(0.5, 4)$ can be modeled by the normal distribution function, then $X = 3$ can be Z-transformed into $Z = m/n$, where m and n are relatively prime, where Z-transformation converts the normal distribution function into the standard normal one. Compute $m + n$.

169. Random Sampling - Part 1.

A bag containing 100 coins is laid out in a floor. To estimate the percent of "quarters" in the bag, a sample of coins is selected at random. The percent of "quarters" in the bag was estimated to be 20%, with an associated margin of error of 2%. If Q is the actual number of quarters in the bag, the most plausible interval that contains Q can be written as either (A, B) or $[A, B]$. Compute $A + B$.

170. Random Sampling - Part 2.

Random Sample	Percent in favor	Margin of Error
X	50%	2.5%
Y	46%	1.1%

The results of two samples of votes for certain candidate are stated above. The samples were randomly selected from the same population and the margin of errors were calculated using the same method. The actual percent in favor of this candidate is more likely to be in which random sample? If the answer is X, write down 100. Otherwise, write down 200.

Part 2

Solution Manual

for 170 Problems

Solution

001.

(a) Yes, this must be true, since $x = y + 3 > y$ because $3 > 0$.

(b) Yes, this must be true, since $x > y > 0$ implies $\sqrt{x} > \sqrt{y} > \sqrt{0}$.

(c) Yes. this must be true. Suppose $x > 0$. Then, $x^2 > 0$. On the other hand, suppose $x < 0$. Then, $x^2 > 0$.

(d) No, this is false. There is a counterexample $(x, y) = (1, -2)$, where $1^2 < (-2)^2$.

(e) Yes, this is true. $|y - x| = |x - y| \geq 0$ and $|x - y| + |y - x| = 0$ imply that $x - y = y - x = 0$. Hence, $x = y$.

(f) Yes, this is true. For all real value of x, $|x - 1| \geq 0$ and $0 > -1$, so $|x - 1| > -1$ for all real value x.

002.

(a) According to the Well-Ordering Principle, a set of whole numbers(or its subsets) always contains the smallest element in it. In fact, $x = 0$. Hence, the sum of the three smallest integers greater than $x = 0$ must be $6 (= 1 + 2 + 3)$.

(b) According to the Well-Ordering Principle, the two smallest elements of the set of primes are 2 and 3. Hence, the sum of these two elements is 5.

(c) Such whole number n can be written as $n = 3k + 2$ where $k \geq 0$. Since $k \geq 0$, we can find the second and third smallest numbers as $n = 3(1) + 2 = 5$ and $n = 3(2) + 2 = 8$. Hence, the sum equals 13.

003.

(a) We simply perform casework. By definition, we know that $|x - y| = x - y$ if $x \geq y$. Otherwise, $|x - y| = y - x$. According to the problem, $x = y + 2$ implies that $x > y$. Hence, $|x - y| = x - y = (y + 2) - y = 2$.

(b) Since $|x - y| = |y - x|$ for any pair of real numbers x and y, $||x - y| - |y - x|| = 0$.

(c) Since $x > 0 > y$, we conclude that $|x - y| = x - y$. Hence, $|x - (x - y) - y| = |0| = 0$.

004.

(a) We perform casework, since we are looking at the absolute-valued expression. First, assume $x \geq 5$. Then, $|x - 5| = x - 5 = 2$ implies that $x = 7$. Check out that $7 > 5$, so $x = 7$ is a valid solution. Second, assume $x < 5$. Then, $|x - 5| = 5 - x = 2$ implies $x = 3$. Check out that $3 < 5$, so $x = 3$ is another valid solution. Hence, the product of all real solutions to the given equation equals $21 (= 7 \times 3)$.

(b) If $|x - 3| = 0$, then the distance between x and 3 is 0. If we paraphrase this, then $x = 3$.

(c) If $||x| - 1| = 2$, we conclude that $|x| - 1 = 2$ or $|x| - 1 = -2$. Since $|x| \geq 0$, we conclude that $|x| = 3$. Hence, there are 2 solutions to the equation.

005.
(a) We perform casework, since we are looking at the absolute-valued equation. First, assume $x \geq 2$. Then, $|2 - x| = x - 2 = 1$ implies $x = 3$. Since $3 \geq 2$, $x = 3$ is a valid solution. Second, assume $x < 2$. Then, $|2 - x| = 2 - x = 1$ implies $x = 1$. Since $1 < 2$, $x = 1$ is another valid solution. Hence, the sum of all real solutions to the given equation equals $4 (= 3 + 1)$.
(b) We notice that $|x| = 4$ or 2. Hence, $x = \pm 4$ and ± 2. The product of all these values must be 64.
(c) Consider $|1 - x| = k \geq 0$. Then, $|k - 1| = 3$ implies that $k = 4$ or -2. Hence, $k = |1 - x| = 4$ results in $x = 5$ and -3. Similarly, $k = |1 - x| = -2$ implies there is no real solution x satisfying the equation. Hence, there is 1 positive real solution.

006.
(a) Look at the inequality carefully. We can rewrite it as a list $\{11, 12, \cdots, 200\}$. This has 1-to-1 correspondence with $\{1, 2, \cdots, 190\}$ by subtracting 10 from each number in the original list. Hence, there are 190 integers in the given interval.
(b) It is easy to check that the smallest possible value of n is $4 = \sqrt{16}$ and the largest possible value of n is $10 = \sqrt{100}$. Hence, we can rewrite the interval as a list $\{4, 5, \cdots, 10\}$. There is 1-to-1 correspondence with $\{1, 2, \cdots, 7\}$ by subtracting 3 from each number in the original list. Hence, there are 7 integers satisfying the given interval.
(c) First, the statement that there are 161 integer values of k satisfying $3^n < k < 3^{n+1}$ can be rewritten as $k = 3^n + 1, 3^n + 2, \cdots, 3^n + 161$. In fact, $3^{n+1} - 1 = 3^n + 161$ implies that $3^{n+1} - 3^n = 162$. Hence, $3(3^n) - 3^n = 162$, so $2(3^n) = 162$. Therefore $3^n = 81$. In particular, $n = 4$.

007. (a) The statement $n - 2 \leq k \leq n + 5$ for integers n and k can be written as $k = n - 2, n - 1, \cdots, n + 4, n + 5$. This range of values corresponds to the integers from $n - 2$ to $n + 5$, inclusive. In other words, it encompasses the numbers $n - 2$, $n - 1$, n, $n + 1$, $n + 2$, $n + 3$, $n + 4$, and $n + 5$. To count the number of integers in this range, we can subtract the lower bound from the upper bound and add 1: $(n + 5) - (n - 2) + 1 = 7 + 1 = 8$. Therefore, there are 8 integer values of k satisfying the given inequality.
(b) The statement $m^2 < k < m^2 + 10$ for integers m and k can be written as $k = m^2 + 1, m^2 + 2, \cdots, m^2 + 9$. This range of values corresponds to the integers from $m^2 + 1$ to $m^2 + 9$, inclusive. In other words, it encompasses the numbers $m^2 + 1$, $m^2 + 2$, $m^2 + 3$, $m^2 + 4$, $m^2 + 5$, $m^2 + 6$, $m^2 + 7$, $m^2 + 8$, and $m^2 + 9$. To count the number of integers in this range, we can subtract the lower bound from the upper bound and add 1: $(m^2 + 9) - (m^2 + 1) + 1 = 8 + 1 = 9$. Therefore, there are 9 integer values of k satisfying the inequality.

008.
(a) Since $k = n^2 + 1, n^2 + 2, \cdots, n^2 + 3n + 1$, we can rewrite it as another list of $\{1, 2, \cdots, 3n + 1\}$. There are 100 numbers in this list, so the last expression satisfies $3n + 1 = 100$. Hence, $n = 33$.
(b) The statement that there are 2002 values of k satisfying $n^3 < k < n^3 + 5n + 3$ can be written as $k = n^3 + 1, n^3 + 2, \cdots, n^3 + 5n + 2$. Then, $5n + 2 = 2002$, so $5n = 2000$. Hence, $n = 400$.

009.
(a) First, $n^2 = 1, 4, \cdots, 1024$ implies that there are 32 possible values of n^2. Since n can be either positive or negative, we conclude that there are 64 possible integer values of n satisfying the given inequality.
(b) Take a square to all numbers in the inequality to conclude that $900 < n^2 < 1000$, which is similar to the inequality shown in (a). Now, $n^2 = 961$ is the only perfect square lying in the interval, and we get $n = \pm 31$. However, since $n > 0$ in the original inequality, we conclude that $n = 31$.
(c)

$$41 < \sqrt{n} < 42$$
$$41^2 < n < 42^2$$

Since n is an integer, $n = 41^2 + 1, 41^2 + 2, \cdots, 42^2 - 1$. The smallest possible value of n can be written as 1682 and the largest possible value of n can be written as 1763. There are $82 (= 1763 - 1682 + 1)$ integer values of n satisfying the given inequality.

010.
(a) As $\sqrt{k}$ and $\sqrt{k+5}$ suggest that $k \geq 0$ and $k \geq -5$, we can start by considering non-negative integer values for k. If we plug in values starting from $k = 0, 1, 2$, and 3, the inequality $\sqrt{k} < \sqrt{k+5}$ holds true for these values. Therefore, there are 4 non-negative integer values of k that satisfy the given inequality.
(b) To solve the inequality $\sqrt{k} < 30 < \sqrt{k+2}$, we can square both sides of the inequality to get rid of the square roots:

$$\sqrt{k} < 30 < \sqrt{k+2}$$
$$k < 900 < k + 2$$

Now, the inequality is equivalent to $k < 900$ and $k + 2 > 900$. So, we have $k < 900$ and $k > 898$. The only integer value of k that satisfies this inequality is $k = 899$.

011.
(a) Let x be the midpoint between -14 and 16. Then, $|16 - x| = |x - (-14)|$ implies that $16 - x = x + 14$. Hence, $x = 1$.
(b) Let x be the point between 5 and 11, satisfying the given condition. According to the equation, $2|11 - x| = |x - 5|$ implies that $2(11 - x) = x - 5$, so $27 = 3x$. Hence, $x = 9$.

012.
(a) $|x - 1| \le 3$ implies that $-3 \le x - 1 \le 3$. Hence, $-2 \le x \le 4$. Therefore, $a + b = (-2) + 4 = 2$.
(b) First, compute the midpoint of 3 and 5 as 4. Then, the distance from 4 to either 3 or 5 equals 1. Hence, $3 < x < 5$ can be written as $|x - 4| < 1$. Hence, $a = 4$ and $L = 1$. The sum must be 5.

013.
(a) Let's perform casework. First, assume $x \ge 0$. Then, $|x - 0| = x - 0 = 5$ implies that $x = 5$. Second, assume $x < 0$. Then, $|x - 0| = 0 - x = 5$ implies that $x = -5$. The product of all these values is -25. Since the problem asks about the absolute value of the product, the answer is 25.
(b) Let's perform casework. First, assume $x < 2$. Then, $|4 - x - 2 + x| = 2$. Second, assume $2 \le x < 4$. Then, $|4 - x - x + 2| = |6 - 2x|$. Third, assume $4 \le x$. Then, $|x - 4 - x + 2| = |-2| = 2$. Hence, there are two real solutions at $2 \le x < 4$. In particular, $|6 - 2x| = 1$ implies that 2.5 or 3.5. Hence, the sum of real solutions equals 6.

014.
(a) Perform casework. Assume $x \ge 2$. Then, $|x - 2| = x - 2 = 2x + 5$ implies that $x = -7$. Since $-7 < 2$, $x = -7$ is invalid. Now, assume $x < 2$. Then, $|x - 2| = 2 - x = 2x + 5$ implies that $x = -1$. Since $-1 < 2$, $x = -1$ is valid. Hence, there is one real solution.
(b) Notice that $2|x - 1| + 3 \ge 3$ for any real x. However, $-2|x - 3| \ge 0$ for any real x. Since the two graphs never meet with one another, there is no real solution.

015.
(a) Perform casework. If $x < 0$, then $|2 - x| = |5x|$ implies that $2 - x = -5x$, so $x = -\frac{1}{2}$, which is valid. If $0 \le x < 2$, then $|2 - x| = |5x|$ implies that $2 - x = 5x$, so $x = \frac{1}{3}$, which is valid. Lastly, if $2 \le x$, then, $x - 2 = 5x$ implies $x = -\frac{1}{2}$, which is invalid. There are two real solutions.
(b) The graph of $y = ||x| - 1|$ is a W-shaped graph. Translate it by 1-unit downward and reflect the graph portion, which is below the x-axis, about the x-axis. Then, the number of intersections between the graph of $y = |||x| - 1| - 1|$ and $y = \frac{1}{2}$ is 6.

016.
(a) First, let N the integer closest to $\sqrt{1000}$. Then, $N < \sqrt{1000} < N+1$. Hence, $N^2 < 1000$ and $(N+1)^2 < 1000$. Hence, look at the values of N^2 closer to 1000, and conclude that $N^2 = 961$. However, 961 is not closer to 1000 than 1024 is. Hence, the closest integer to $\sqrt{1000}$ must be 32.
(b) We look at perfect cubes near 730. We notice that $9^3 < 730 < 10^3$. Since 9^3 is closer to 730 than 10^3 is, we approximate 9 as the closest integer to $\sqrt[3]{730}$.

017.
$\sqrt{2}$ is smaller than 2 and $\sqrt{1025}$ is greater than 32. Hence, $\sqrt{2} < 2 < 32 < \sqrt{1025}$. Hence, there are 31 integer values of p satisfying the inequality.

018.
(a)

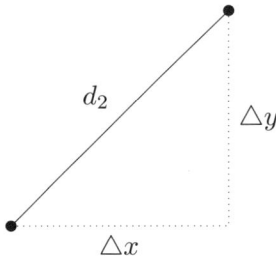

As shown in the figure above, since 2000 is fixed, we simply compute $d_1 = 1001 - 1000$.
(b)

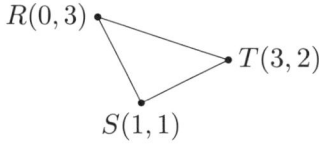

Let d_2 be the distance between $(5,8)$ and $(2,5)$. Then,

$$d_2 = \sqrt{(5-2)^2 + (8-5)^2}$$
$$= \sqrt{18}$$

Hence, $d_2^2 = 18$.

019.
(a) Notice that $\overline{RS} \perp \overline{ST}$, as shown in the figure below.

Also, using the distance formula, we get

$$RS = \sqrt{(1-0)^2 + (1-3)^2}$$
$$= \sqrt{1+4}$$
$$ST = \sqrt{(3-1)^2 + (2-1)^2}$$
$$= \sqrt{4+1}$$

Hence, the area of this right triangle equals $\frac{5}{2}$, so the answer is 7.

(b) The area of a triangle that can be found by drawing auxiliary lines or shoelace theorem. First, if we draw auxiliary lines (both horizontal lines and vertical lines) passing through the points $(4,1)$, $(1,3)$ and $(2,5)$, we get a large rectangle of area 12. Then, there are three extra triangles of area 1, 3, and 4, that should be excluded, as illustrated below.

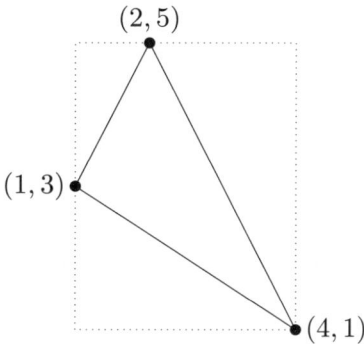

Hence, the area of $\triangle ABC$ must be $12 - (1 + 4 + 3) = 4$. Second, the shoelace theorem can be applied to $(4,1)$, $(1,3)$ and $(2,5)$. Look at the following columns and rows of numbers.

4	1
1	3
2	5
4	1

The key idea about shoelace theorem is that we write whichever coordinates we write first time again in the last row. Just like how shoelace looks, we take the sum of product of short diagonals whose directions go southeastward and subtract the sum of product of short diagonals whose directions go southwestward. In other words,
$(4 \cdot 3 + 1 \cdot 5 + 2 \cdot 1) - (1 \cdot 1 + 3 \cdot 2 + 5 \cdot 4)$. We take the absolute value of the given expression, and divide it by 2 to get the area of a triangle, which equals 4.

020.

(a) When we use distance formula, we look at horizontal and vertical cases, separately. First, $m = \dfrac{6+2}{2} = 4$. Second, $n = \dfrac{10+(-8)}{2} = 1$. Hence, $m+n = 4+1 = 5$.

(b) If $(\sqrt{3}, 1)$ is rotated 90° counterclockwise about the origin, then its coordinates are determined by the perpendicular line to the graph. Since the original point has the associated slope of $\dfrac{1}{\sqrt{3}}$, the perpendicular line to this must have the slope of $-\sqrt{3}$. Hence, the resulting point must be $(-1, \sqrt{3})$. Therefore, $\dfrac{b^2}{a^2} = 3$.

021. Let's go over this case in horizontal and vertical cases, separately. First, m is between 2 and 6, in a horizontal line. According to the condition, $6 - m : m - 2 = 3 : 2$ implies $3m - 6 = 12 - 2m$, so $5m = 18$. Hence, $m = \dfrac{18}{5}$. Second, n is between -8 and 10, in a vertical line. According to the condition, $10 - n : n - (-8) = 2 : 3$ implies $30 - 3n = 2n + 16$, so $5n = 14$. Hence, $n = \dfrac{14}{5}$. Thus, $m + n = \dfrac{32}{5}$. Therefore, $p + q = 32 + 5 = 37$.

022.

(a) Let $(a, 0)$ and $(b, 0)$ be the points on the x-axis. Using the Pythagoras theorem, we can easily find out that $(a, b) = (3 - \sqrt{13}, 3 + \sqrt{13})$ or $(3 + \sqrt{13}, 3 - \sqrt{13})$. Then, $a + b = 3 - \sqrt{13} + 3 + \sqrt{13} = 6$.

(b) Let $A(x, y)$ and $B(m, n)$ be the third vertices of the equilateral triangle. Then, using $30° - 60° - 90°$ triangle property, we can easily conclude that $A = (2\sqrt{3}, 2)$ or $(-2\sqrt{3}, 2)$; likewise, $B = (-2\sqrt{3}, 2)$ or $(2\sqrt{3}, 2)$, respectively. Hence, the sum of x, y, m and n must be 4.

023.

Solution 1 Let the perpendicular line to the given line, passing through $(4, 2)$, be $y = \dfrac{1}{2}(x-4) + 2 = \dfrac{1}{2}x$. The intersection point between $4x + 2y = 11$ and $2y = x$ can be easily found by substitution. In particular, $x = \dfrac{11}{5}$ and $y = \dfrac{11}{10}$. Hence, the distance between $(4, 2)$ and $\left(\dfrac{11}{5}, \dfrac{11}{10}\right)$ can be found by $\dfrac{9\sqrt{5}}{10}$. Hence, the answer must be $24(= 9 + 5 + 10)$.

Solution 2 According to the distance formula between a point and a line, we use

$$\dfrac{|4(4) + 2(2) - 11|}{\sqrt{4^2 + 2^2}} = \dfrac{9}{\sqrt{20}} = \dfrac{9\sqrt{5}}{10}$$

Hence, the answer must be $24(= 9 + 5 + 10)$.

024.

(a) First, we must find the x-intercept and y-intercept of the given graphs. By plugging $x = 0$, we get the y-intercept of 4. Also, by plugging $y = 0$, we get the x-intercept of 3. Hence, the area of triangle formed by the x-intercept, y-intercept, and the origin can easily be found by $\frac{1}{2} \times 3 \times 4 = 6$ square units.

(b) Since the triangle formed by (m,n), $(m,0)$ and $(0,0)$ is similar to $3:4:5$ triangle. We first compute the distance between $(0,0)$ and (m,n) as the distance between the origin and the line $4x + 3y = 12$, which equals $\frac{12}{5}$. Hence, the similarity ratio suggests that $(m,n) = \left(\frac{48}{25}, \frac{36}{25}\right)$. Hence, $m + n = \frac{84}{25}$, so $p + q = 109$.

025.

(a) Let's compute the x-intercepts first by plugging $y = 0$ into the given expression. Then, $x^2 = 4$ implies $x = \pm 2$. Likewise, we get the y-intercept of 64 by plugging $x = 0$ into the given expression. Hence, $P = -2 \cdot 2 \cdot 64 = -256$. Thus, $|P| = |-256| = 256$.

(b) It is easy to check that $(m,n) = \left(0, \frac{64}{3}\right)$. Hence, $m + n = \frac{64}{3}$, so $p + q = 64 + 3 = 67$.

026.

(a) Due to the symmetry of the graph about the x-axis, if (a,b) is a point on the graph, then $(a,-b)$ must also be on it. Therefore, if we know that $(1,5)$ is on the graph, we can conclude that $(1,-5)$ is also on the graph. Thus, to find $|x + y|$, we can calculate $|1 + (-5)|$, which equals $|-4|$, resulting in $|x + y| = 4$.

(b) Given that $(2,7)$ is the point of symmetry, we can deduce that for any point on the graph, $(2 - r, 7 - s)$, there will be a symmetric point $(2 + r, 7 + s)$ on the graph. Therefore, if we know that $(1,5)$ is on the graph, we can determine that $r = 1$ and $s = 2$ since $(1,5)$ corresponds to $(2-1, 7-2)$. Consequently, we find that $(3,9)$ is also on the graph. Thus, we can conclude that $xy = 27$.

027. Since $(1,5)$ passes through the line perpendicular to $y = \frac{1}{2}x$, then (a,b) is also on the line $y = -2(x - 1) + 5 = -2x + 7$. Finding the intersection point between $y = -2x + 7$ and $y = \frac{1}{2}x$, we get $(x,y) = \left(\frac{14}{5}, \frac{7}{5}\right)$. Also, since the midpoint of (a,b) and $(1,5)$ is on the graph of $y = \frac{1}{2}x$, we conclude that $\left(\frac{a+1}{2}, \frac{b+5}{2}\right)$ is on the graph of $y = \frac{1}{2}x$. Hence,

$$\left(\frac{14}{5}, \frac{7}{5}\right) = \left(\frac{a+1}{2}, \frac{b+5}{2}\right)$$

Hence, $a + b = \frac{12}{5}$. Thus, $m + n = 17$.

028. Since $|x|$ and x^2 take away negative signs for all values of x, if $(2,2)$ is on the graph, then $(-2,2)$ is also on the graph. Hence, the answer is $(-2)^2 = 4$.

029. If (x,y) is in the 2nd Quadrant, then $x < 0$ and $y > 0$. Now, $|-x| > 0$ implies that $-|-x| < 0$. Similarly, $|y|^2 > 0$ for $y < 0$. Hence, the point $(-|-x|, |y|^2) = (-, +)$ is also in the 2nd Quadrant. Therefore, $n = 2$.

030. The vertical height of the triangle can be found by the distance between $(-3, -4)$ and $(-3, 4)$, which equals 8. Likewise, the horizontal width of the triangle can be found by the distance between $(-3, 4)$ and $(3, 4)$, which equals 6. Hence, the area of right triangle can be found by $\frac{1}{2} \times 6 \times 8 = 24$.

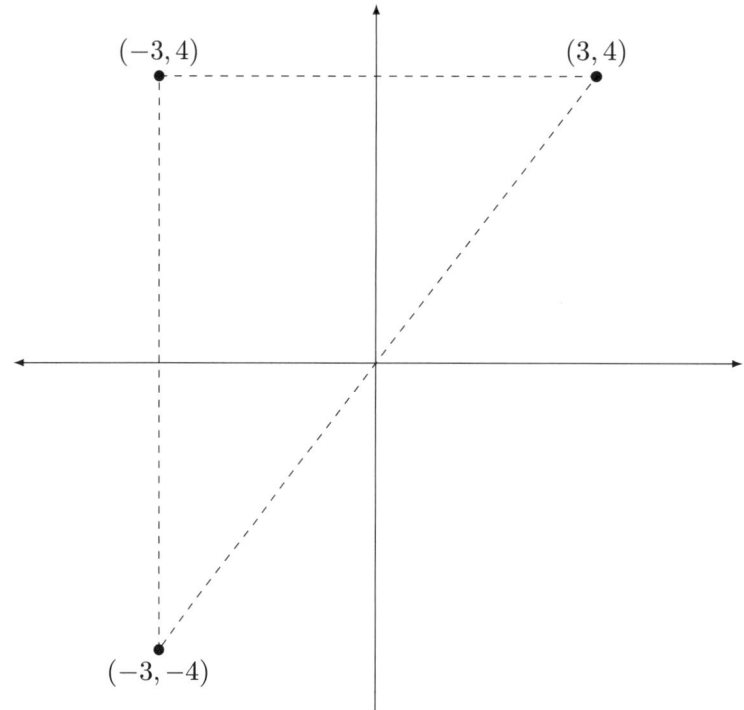

031. We can determine that the perpendicular bisector of the line segment connecting $(3, 7)$ and $(6, 4)$ has a slope of 1. Therefore, we can represent this perpendicular bisector as a line in the form of $y = x + b$. As it passes through the midpoint of $(3, 7)$ and $(6, 4)$, it must also pass through the point $(4.5, 5.5)$. By substituting these coordinates into the equation, we find that $b = 1$. Consequently, the equation of the perpendicular bisector is $y = mx + b$, which simplifies to $y = x + 1$. This equation tells us that the slope (m) plus the intercept (b) equals 2, as $m + b = 2$.

032.
(a) A line equation $2x - 3y = 5$ can turn into $y = \dfrac{2}{3}x - \dfrac{5}{3}$. Hence, the perpendicular line to it must have the slope of $-\dfrac{3}{2}$. Let's write the line equation into $y = -\dfrac{3}{2}x + b$. Since it passes through $(2, 3)$, we can write it as $3 = -\dfrac{3}{2}(2) + b$ to conclude that $b = 6$. Thus, $y = mx + b = -\dfrac{3}{2}x + 6$. The answer must be $|-\dfrac{3}{2} \times 6| = 9$.
(b) Since the line is parallel to $3x - 5y = 1$, then $(a, b) = (3, 5)$. Thus, $3(1) - 5(3) = -12 = c$. Hence, $|c| = 12$.

033. To locate the intersection point between the line $x = 3$ and $y = -5$, we find it at $(3, -5)$. Now, since this point needs to be reflected about the line $y = x$, we can achieve this reflection by swapping the x and y coordinates. Thus, the reflected point (m, n) becomes $(-5, 3)$. Consequently, to calculate $n - m$, we find the difference between 3 and -5, which equals 8.

034.
(a) Since the line is parallel to $3x - y = 4$, then it must be in the form of $3x - y = n$. Substitute $(2, 4)$ into the given form to find out $3(2) - 4 = n = 2$. Hence, we get the line equation of $3x - y = 2$. Since 3 and 1 are already relatively prime, we conclude that $C = n = 2$.
(b) If $2x + y = 4$ is reflected about the x-axis, then it turns into $2x - y = 4$. Likewise, if $2x - y = 4$ is reflected about the y-axis, then it turns into $-2x - y = 4$, which is reflected about the x-axis to result in $-2x + y = 4$. Hence, all four lines form a rhombus whose x-coordinates are either 2 or -2 and y-coordinates are either 4 or -4. Hence, the area of rhombus equals 16 square units.

035.
(a) The vertical line that contains $(-5, -3)$ can be written as $x = -5$. Since $x = -5$ is 5 units away from the origin, the distance from the origin to the line must be 5.
(b) Since a rectangle is cyclic, the circumdiameter equals $\sqrt{3^2 + 5^2} = \sqrt{34}$. Hence, the answer is 34.

036. If three points are collinear, like $(3, 4)$ and $(0, 7)$, it means there's a direct path between them. In this case, going from $(3, 4)$ to $(0, 7)$ implies moving 3 units to the left and 3 units upward. So, to find the value of a in the equation $2a + 1$, we consider that it should represent a 1-unit leftward shift from 0. Therefore, $2a + 1$ must equal -1, and solving for a yields $a = -1$. The absolute value of a is 1.

037.

Solution 1 Using the distance formula between a point and a line, we get
$d = \dfrac{|8(0) + 5(0) - 40|}{\sqrt{8^2 + 5^2}} = \dfrac{40}{\sqrt{89}}$. Hence, $d^2 = \dfrac{1600}{89}$, so $1600 + 89 = 1689$.

Solution 2 The shortest path from the origin to the line $8x + 5y = 40$ equals the altitude from the origin to the hypotenuse of a triangle formed by the origin, x-intercept, and y-intercept. Computing the area of a triangle by multiplying the base and height, we get

$$\frac{1}{2} \times 5 \times 8 = \frac{1}{2} \times \sqrt{89} \times d$$

Hence, $d = \dfrac{40}{\sqrt{89}}$. Therefore, $d^2 = \dfrac{1600}{89}$.

038.

The altitude from the origin to the line $8x + 5y = 120$ is three times that from the origin to the line $8x + 5y = 40$. Hence, the distance from the line $8x + 5y = 40$ to the line $8x + 5y = 120$ is twice the altitude from the origin to the line $8x + 5y = 40$. Therefore, $d = \dfrac{80}{\sqrt{89}}$. Therefore, $d^2 = \dfrac{6400}{89}$. Hence, the answer is $6400 + 89 = 6489$.

039.

Since two lines are equivalent, $\dfrac{4}{A} = \dfrac{2}{B} = \dfrac{5}{20}$. Hence, $A = 16$ and $B = 8$. The product of A and B equals 128.

040.

(a) According to the given condition, the slope of a line perpendicular to L_1 is a negative reciprocal of $-\dfrac{4}{7}$. Hence, $\dfrac{m}{n} = \dfrac{7}{4}$. Now, let $m = 7k$ and $n = 4k$ for some integer k. Then, $90 < m + n = 11k < 100$ indicates that $11k = 99$. Hence, $m + n = 99$.

(b) One of the lines can be written as $y = m(x - 1) + 2$, while the other can be written as $y = (3 - m)(x - 1) + 2$. Hence, at $x = 4$, we get $y_1 = 3m + 2$ and $y_2 = (3 - m)3 + 2$. Hence, $y_1 + y_2 = 13$.

041.

(a) It is a function of x, so the answer is 1.
(b) It is not a function of x, so the answer is 0.
(c) It is not a function of x, so the answer is 0.
(d) It is a function of x, so the answer is 1.

Hence, the number we are interested in is $\overline{1001}_{(2)}$, which can be converted into $1(2^3) + 0(2^2) + 0(2^1) + 1 = 9$ in base-10.

042.

Step 1. Find all critical points by finding the intersection points of the given inequalities, i.e., $(0,0)$, $(0,2)$, $(3,0)$ and $\left(\dfrac{18}{11}, \dfrac{20}{11}\right)$.

Step 2. Substitute the given points inside the optimizing expression.

$$3x + 2y = 3(0) + 2(0) = 0$$
$$= 3(0) + 2(2) = 4$$
$$= 3(3) + 2(0) = 9$$
$$= 3\left(\dfrac{18}{11}\right) + 2\left(\dfrac{20}{11}\right) = \dfrac{94}{11}$$

Hence, the maximum value of 9 is reached at $(3,0)$.

043.

Step 1. Find all critical points by finding the intersection points of the given inequalities, i.e., $(0,0)$, $(0,6)$, $(3,0)$ and $\left(\dfrac{6}{11}, \dfrac{63}{11}\right)$.

Step 2. Substitute the given points inside the optimizing expression.

$$5x + 3y = 5(0) + 3(0) = 0$$
$$= 5(0) + 3(6) = 18$$
$$= 5(3) + 3(0) = 15$$
$$= 5\left(\dfrac{6}{11}\right) + 3\left(\dfrac{63}{11}\right) = \dfrac{219}{11}$$

Hence, the answer must be 230.

044.

Step 1. Find all critical points by finding the intersection points of the given inequalities, i.e., $(0,2)$, $(0,4)$, $(2,2)$, $(2,3.5)$, and $(1,4)$.

Step 2. Substitute the given points inside the optimizing expression.

$$5x + 3y = 5(0) + 3(2) = 6$$
$$= 5(0) + 3(4) = 12$$
$$= 5(2) + 3(2) = 16$$
$$= 5(2) + 3(3.5) = 20.5$$
$$= 5(1) + 3(4) = 17$$

Hence, the maximum value of $\dfrac{41}{2}$ is reached at $(2, 3.5)$. The answer must be 43.

045.

Step 1. Find all critical points by finding the intersection points of the given inequalities, i.e., $(2, 0)$, $(5, 0)$, $\left(\dfrac{20}{19}, \dfrac{45}{19}\right)$.

Step 2. Substitute the given points inside the optimizing expression.

$$x + y = 2 + 0 = 2 < 5$$
$$= 0 + 5 = 5$$
$$= \frac{20}{19} + \frac{45}{19} = \frac{65}{19} < 5$$

Hence, the maximum value must be 5.

046.

There are 13 solutions in total. We perform casework on each x-value.

x	y
0	$0, 1, 2, 3$
1	$0, 1, 2$
2	$0, 1$
3	$0, 1$
4	0
5	0

047.

There are 11 solutions in total. We perform casework on each x-value.

x	y
0	$0, 1, 2$
1	$0, 1$
2	$0, 1$
3	$0, 1$
4	0
5	0

048.

(a)

$$\begin{bmatrix} 1 & 0 \\ 0 & 1 \end{bmatrix} \begin{bmatrix} 0 & 1 \\ 0 & 1 \end{bmatrix} \begin{bmatrix} 0 & 1 \\ 1 & 0 \end{bmatrix} \begin{bmatrix} 1 & 0 \\ 1 & 0 \end{bmatrix} \begin{bmatrix} 4 & 3 \\ 2 & 1 \end{bmatrix} = \begin{bmatrix} 1 & 0 \\ 0 & 1 \end{bmatrix} \begin{bmatrix} 0 & 1 \\ 0 & 1 \end{bmatrix} \begin{bmatrix} 0 & 1 \\ 1 & 0 \end{bmatrix} \begin{bmatrix} 4 & 3 \\ 4 & 3 \end{bmatrix}$$
$$= \begin{bmatrix} 1 & 0 \\ 0 & 1 \end{bmatrix} \begin{bmatrix} 0 & 1 \\ 0 & 1 \end{bmatrix} \begin{bmatrix} 4 & 3 \\ 4 & 3 \end{bmatrix}$$
$$= \begin{bmatrix} 1 & 0 \\ 0 & 1 \end{bmatrix} \begin{bmatrix} 4 & 3 \\ 4 & 3 \end{bmatrix}$$
$$= \begin{bmatrix} 4 & 3 \\ 4 & 3 \end{bmatrix}$$

Hence, the sum of all entries is 14.

(b)

$$\begin{bmatrix} 1 & 0 \\ 0 & 1 \end{bmatrix} \begin{bmatrix} 0 & 1 \\ 0 & 1 \end{bmatrix} \begin{bmatrix} 1 & 1 \\ 0 & 0 \end{bmatrix} \begin{bmatrix} 0 & 1 \\ 1 & 0 \end{bmatrix} = \begin{bmatrix} 1 & 0 \\ 0 & 1 \end{bmatrix} \begin{bmatrix} 0 & 1 \\ 0 & 1 \end{bmatrix} \begin{bmatrix} 1 & 1 \\ 0 & 0 \end{bmatrix}$$
$$= \begin{bmatrix} 1 & 0 \\ 0 & 1 \end{bmatrix} \begin{bmatrix} 0 & 0 \\ 0 & 0 \end{bmatrix}$$
$$= \begin{bmatrix} 0 & 0 \\ 0 & 0 \end{bmatrix}$$

Hence, the sum of all entries is 0.

049.

(a)

$$\begin{bmatrix} 1 & -1 \\ -1 & 1 \end{bmatrix} \begin{bmatrix} 4 & 3 \\ 2 & 1 \end{bmatrix} = \begin{bmatrix} 2 & 2 \\ -2 & -2 \end{bmatrix}$$

Hence, the sum of all entries is 0.

(b)

$$\begin{bmatrix} 5 & 6 \\ 4 & 5 \end{bmatrix}^{-1} = \frac{1}{25-24} \begin{bmatrix} 5 & -6 \\ -4 & 5 \end{bmatrix} = \begin{bmatrix} 5 & -6 \\ -4 & 5 \end{bmatrix}$$

Hence, the sum of all entries is 0.

050.

(a)
$$\begin{bmatrix} 1 & 0 & 0 \\ 1 & 0 & 0 \\ 0 & -1 & 2 \end{bmatrix} \begin{bmatrix} 1 & 2 & 3 \\ 0 & 0 & 0 \\ -1 & -2 & -3 \end{bmatrix} = \begin{bmatrix} 1 & 2 & 3 \\ 1 & 2 & 3 \\ -2 & -4 & -6 \end{bmatrix}$$

Hence, the sum of all entries is 0.

(b)
$$\begin{bmatrix} 0 & 1 & 0 \\ 1 & 0 & 0 \\ 0 & 0 & 1 \end{bmatrix} \begin{bmatrix} 1 & 2 & 3 \\ 0 & 0 & 0 \\ -3 & -2 & -1 \end{bmatrix} = \begin{bmatrix} 0 & 0 & 0 \\ 1 & 2 & 3 \\ -3 & -2 & -1 \end{bmatrix}$$

Hence, the sum of all entries is 0.

051.

(a) $x^2 - 15x - 16 = (x - 16)(x + 1) = 0$, so $x = 16, -1$. The difference is 17.

(b) $x^2 - 24x + 143 = (x - 13)(x - 11) = 0$, so $x = 11, 13$. The difference is 2.

(c) $x^2 - 17x + 52 = (x - 4)(x - 13) = 0$, so $x = 4, 13$. The difference is 9.

(d) $x^2 - 12x - 28 = (x - 14)(x + 2) = 0$, so $x = 14, -2$. The difference is 16.

(e) $x^2 - 5x - 84 = (x - 12)(x + 7) = 0$, so $x = 12, -7$. The difference is 19.

052.

(a)
$$3x^2 - 6x + 12 = 3(x^2 - 2x + 1 - 1) + 12$$
$$= 3(x^2 - 2x + 1) - 3 + 12$$
$$= 3(x - 1)^2 + 9$$

Hence, $a = 3$, $p = 1$, and $q = 9$. Therefore, $3 + 1 + 9 = 13$.

(b)

Solution 1 The vertex form can be written as $y = a(x-1)^2 + 4$. Since it passes through $(2,6)$, $a(2-1)^2 + 4 = 6$ implies $a = 2$. Hence, $y = 2(x-1)^2 + 4 = 2(x^2 - 2x + 1) + 4 = 2x^2 - 4x + 6$. Hence, $(a,b,c) = (2, -4, 6)$, implying that the sum is 4.

Solution 2 Given $y = ax^2 + bx + c$, $a + b + c$ can be reached by plugging $x = 1$. Since the graph passes through the point $(1, 4)$, we safely conclude that $a + b + c = 4$.

053.

(a) First, $f(x) = -6x^2 + 36x = -6x(x - 6)$ implies that the axis of symmetry is $x = 3$. Since the vertex is located at the axis of symmetry, plug $x = 3$ to get $y = -6(3)(-3) = 54$. Thus, the maximum value of $f(x)$ is 54 at $x = 3$.

(b) First, $y = 4x^2 - 16x = 4x(x - 4)$. The minimum value of y can be reached at $x = 2$. In particular, $y = 4(2)(2 - 4) = -16$ is the minimum value. Since $M = -16$, the absolute value of M is 16.

054.

(a) The associated discriminant must be a perfect square, so $p^2 - 8p = q^2$. Hence, $(p-4)^2 - q^2 = 16$. Thus, $(p - 4 - q)(p - 4 + q) = 16$ implies that $(p - 4 - q, p - 4 + q) = (2, 8)$, $(4, 4)$, $(8, 2)$, $(-2, -8)$, $(-4, -4)$, and $(-8, -2)$. Going over all cases, we get $p = 9, 8, 0, -1$. Hence, there are 4 distinct values of p.

(b) Since the curve is tangent to the x-axis, it means that $x^2 + px + (p + 3)$ has one repeated real solution. In other words, the associated discriminant is 0. Hence, $p^2 - 4(p + 3) = p^2 - 4p - 12 = (p - 6)(p + 2) = 0$. The positive difference of p-values equals $6 - (-2) = 8$.

055.

(a)
$$x^2 - 2kx + k^2 = 3 + x$$
$$x^2 - (2k+1)x + (k^2 - 3) = 0$$
$$(2k+1)^2 - 4(k^2 - 3) \geq 0$$
$$4k^2 + 4k + 1 - 4k^2 + 12 \geq 0$$
$$4k + 13 \geq 0$$
$$k \geq -\frac{13}{4}$$

Hence, $|K| = \frac{13}{4}$, so the answer is $17 (= 13 + 4)$.

(b)
$$(-x + p)^2 = x + p$$
$$x^2 - 2px + p^2 = x + p$$
$$x^2 - (2p+1)x + (p^2 - p) = 0$$
$$(2p+1)^2 - 4(p^2 - p) < 0$$
$$4p^2 + 4p + 1 - 4p^2 + 4p < 0$$
$$8p + 1 < 0$$
$$p < -\frac{1}{8}$$

Hence, $P = -\frac{1}{8}$. Thus, $|\frac{1}{P}| = 8$.

056.

(a) $x(x-3) < 4$ implies that $x^2 - 3x - 4 < 0$. Hence, $(x-4)(x+1) < 0$. Thus, $-1 < x < 4$. Since $m = -1$ and $n = 4$, $m + n = 3$.

(b) $x^2 < 4x + 21$ implies that $x^2 - 4x - 21 < 0$. Hence, $(x+3)(x-7) < 0$. Thus, $-3 < x < 7$. Since $m = -3$ and $n = 7$, $m + n = 4$.

057.

(a) Paraphrase the statement that $y < 0$ only when $3 < x < k$ into $(x-3)(x-k) < 0$. Since $y = x^2 - px + 12$ satisfies such inequality,

$$x^2 - px + 12 = (x-3)(x-k)$$
$$x^2 - px + 12 = x^2 - (3+k)x + 3k$$

Solving $3k = 12$ and $p = 3 + k$, we can conclude that $k = 4$ and $p = 7$. Thus, the product of these values is 28.

(b) Since the curve equation can turn into $(x-2)^2 + (y-1)^2 = 1$, we simply substitute $y = 2x - 1$, found by the condition that the line passes through both $(0, -1)$ and $(1, 1)$. Hence,

$$(x-2)^2 + (2x-2)^2 = 1$$
$$x^2 - 4x + 4 + 4(x^2 - 2x + 1) = 1$$
$$5x^2 - 12x + 8 = 1$$
$$5x^2 - 12x + 7 = 0$$
$$(5x - 7)(x - 1) = 0$$

Thus, $x = \dfrac{7}{5}$ or $x = 1$. At $x = \dfrac{7}{5}$, $y = 2\left(\dfrac{7}{5}\right) - 1 = \dfrac{14}{5} - 1 = \dfrac{9}{5}$. Hence, the sum of the coordinates equals $\dfrac{16}{5}$, so the answer is 21.

058.

(a) Since $(x-2)^2 + (y+3)^2 = 4^2$ equals $x^2 - Ax + y^2 + By = C$, we expand the first equation to find out $A = 4$, $B = 6$ and $C = 3$. Hence, the sum equals 13.

(b)

$$(x-3)^2 + (y+4)^2 = 25$$
$$(x-3)^2 + 4^2 = 25$$
$$(x-3)^2 = 9$$
$$|x - 3| = 3$$
$$x = 6, 0$$

The sum of the x-intercepts is $6 + 0 = 6$.

059.

(a)
$$x^2 - 6x + 9 + y^2 + 8y + 16 = -11 + 25$$
$$(x-3)^2 + (y+4)^2 = 14$$
$$(x-3)^2 + (y+4)^2 = (\sqrt{14})^2$$

Hence, $n = 14$.

(b)
Step 1. The smaller circle has the length of $4\sqrt{2}$ due to an isosceles triangle property. Hence, the area must be $(4\sqrt{2})^2 = 32$ square units.

Step 2. The larger circle has the length of 8 since it is equal to the length of the diameter of circle. Hence, the area must be $8^2 = 64$ square units.

The difference between the two areas equals 32 square units.

060. Since $3 - 2i$ is a solution to $x^2 + ax + b = 0$ where a and b are integers, then $\overline{3 - 2i} = 3 + 2i$. Hence, $b = (3 - 2i)(3 + 2i) = 9 + 4 = 13$.

061. Since the problem provides with the solution $x = \sqrt{3}$, we simply substitute the given value $x = \sqrt{3}$ into the original expression to conclude that $x^3 - 3x + c = 0$ implies that $c = 0$.

062.
$$\frac{1+i}{2-i} = \frac{(1+i)(2+i)}{(2-i)(2+i)}$$
$$= \frac{1+3i}{5}$$

Hence, $a + b + c = 9$.

063.
$$x^2 + 1 = 10x$$
$$x + \frac{1}{x} = 10$$

since $x \neq 0$. Suppose $x = 0$ for the sake of contradiction. Then, $0 + 1 = 10(0)$, which is false. Hence, the original assumption must have been false. Therefore, we know that $x \neq 0$. Thus, the answer to our problem is 10.

064. According to the given condition, $(-4)^2 - 4c < 0$ by discriminant. Hence, $16 < 4c$ implies that $4 < c$. By the Well-Ordering Principle, we know that the minimum possible value of c equals 5.

065. By Viete's formula, we know that $a + b = 3$ and $ab = -1$. Then, $a^2 + b^2 = (a+b)^2 - 2ab = 9 + 2 = 11$. Hence, $a^4 + b^4 = (a^2 + b^2)^2 - 2a^2b^2 = 121 - 2(-1)^2 = 119$.

066. Since $x^2 - 6x + 5 \leq 0$, we can turn it into $(x-1)(x-5) \leq 0$, so $1 \leq x \leq 5$. Since x is an integer, we conclude that $x = 1, 2, 3, 4, 5$. Thus, the sum of all these values equals 15.

067. If $y = x^2$ is reflected about the y-axis, then it is still $y = x^2$. If it is translated 2 units left and 3 units up, then $y = (x+2)^2 + 3$. Hence, the vertex must be $(-2, 3)$. Thus, $m + n = (-2) + 3 = 1$.

068.
(a) Complete the square to find out $y = x^2 - 6x - 1 = (x^2 - 6x + 9) - 10 = (x-3)^2 - 10$. Hence, the minimum value equals -10 at $x = 3$.
(b) The graphs of $|x| + |y| = 1$ and $y = x^2 - 6x + 1$ meet at a point on the fourth quadrant. The portion of the graph of $|x| + |y| = 1$ meets the curve at $y = x - 1$, so we solve the system of equations $x - 1 = x^2 - 6x + 1$ to conclude that $x = \frac{7-\sqrt{41}}{2}$. Hence, the minimum value of y occurs at $y = x - 1 = \frac{7-\sqrt{41}}{2} - 1 = \frac{5-\sqrt{41}}{2}$. Thus, $a = 5$, $b = 41$, and $c = 2$. Therefore, $a + b + c = 48$.

069.
(a) $\deg(f(x)) = 1$
(b) $\deg(g(x)) = 2$
(c) $\deg(s(x)) = 2$

070. There is a second layer with the fixed difference of 6. Since there are two layers of differences, the degree of the polynomial is 2. The standard difference of $y = x^2$ in the last layer is 2, but the given difference in the problem is 6, which is 3 times the standard difference. Hence, $a_n = a_2 = 3$ and $n = 2$. Therefore, the product of a_n and n equals 6.

071.

$$x^3 - 27 = x^3 - 3^3$$
$$= (x-3)(x^2 + 3x + 9)$$

Hence, $x = 3$. The solutions to $x^2 + 3x + 9 = 0$ are all complex since $b^2 - 4ac = 3^2 - 4(9) < 0$. Hence, there is only one real solution.

072.

$$x^3 + 64 = x^3 + 4^3$$
$$= (x+4)(x^2 - 4x + 16)$$

It is obvious that $x = -4$. However, the solutions to $x^2 - 4x + 16 = 0$ are all complex since $b^2 - 4ac = (-4)^2 - 4(16) < 0$. Hence, there is one real solution.

073. Using the Integer Root Theorem, try $x = \pm 1, \pm 2, \pm 3, \pm 4, \pm 6$, and ± 12. It is easy to check that $x = 1$, $x = -3$, and $x = 4$ work out. Therefore, $|r| + |s| + |t| = 1 + 3 + 4 = 8$.

074. Using the Integer Root Theorem, try signed factors of 70. Try first few terms, i.e., $x = \pm 1, \pm 2, \pm 5, \pm 7, \pm 10, \cdots$. Luckily, we can find out that $x = 2$ is a zero of $x^3 - 4x^2 - 31x + 70 = 0$. Use synthetic division to find out that it turns out to be $(x-2)(x^2 - 2x - 35) = 0$. Hence, $x = 7$ and $x = -5$. Therefore, $|r| + |s| + |t| = 2 + 5 + 7 = 14$.

075. Using the Integer Root Theorem, we try out $x = \pm 1, \pm 2, \pm 3, \pm 6$. It works out that $x = 3$ is a zero. However, $x^3 - 4x^2 + 5x - 6 = (x-3)(x^2 - x + 2) = 0$ implies that there is only one real value $x = 3$. Hence, $k = 3$.

076. At $x = 0$, the cubic expression is positive. At $x = 1$, the cubic expression is negative. The Intermediate Value Theorem implies that the only rational solution can be $1/2$. Using synthetic division, we get

$$2x^3 - 5x^2 - 14x + 8 = (2x - 1)(x^2 - 2x - 8)$$
$$= (2x - 1)(x - 4)(x + 2) = 0$$

At $x = \frac{1}{2}$, 4, and -2, the cubic equation turns into 0. The sum of positive real roots can be written as $9/2$, so the answer is 11.

077. The only rational solutions we can check by rational root theorem are $\pm\frac{1}{2}$, $\pm\frac{1}{3}$, or $\pm\frac{1}{6}$. Now, $x = \frac{1}{2}$ is the solution to the equation, so the synthetic division results in $(2x - 1)(3x^2 - 2x - 1) = (2x - 1)(3x - 1)(x + 1) = 0$. In fact, all the solutions that appear in this equation are rational and they all apear in the possible rational zero candidates. Now, the sum of positive real roots is $\frac{1}{2} + \frac{1}{3} = \frac{5}{6}$. Hence, the answer is 11.

078. Solving $n^2(n - 2)(n - 4) < 0$ by graphing it, we easily get that $2 < n < 4$ is the only interval that satisfies the given inequality. Hence, the only integer value n that satisfies the given inequality is $n = 3$.

079. By the remainder theorem, we can write $x^3 + 5x + 4 = (x - 1)Q(x) + r$. At $x = 1$, the left-hand side of the equation turns into 10, while the right-hand side of it becomes r. Hence, the remainder we want is 10.

080. Possible rational roots can be manually found by

$$\frac{\pm 1, \pm 2, \pm 5, \pm 10}{\pm 1, \pm 2}$$

Hence, the solutions that work out are $\pm 1, \pm 2, \pm 5, \pm 10, \pm 1/2, \pm 5/2$.

081.

$$f(-x) = f(2x)$$
$$-2x^3 - 5x^2 - 10x - 1 = 16x^3 - 20x^2 + 20x - 1$$
$$18x^3 - 15x^2 + 30x = 0$$

Hence, the sum of solutions are $\frac{15}{18} = \frac{5}{6}$. Therefore, $m + n = 11$.

082.

$$(r+1)(s+1)(t+1) = -(-1-r)(-1-s)(-1-t)$$
$$= -((-1)^3 - 5(-1)^2 + 3(-1) - 1)$$
$$= -(-10)$$
$$= 10$$

083.

$$(r^2-1)(s^2-1)(t^2-1) = (r-1)(s-1)(t-1)(r+1)(s+1)(t+1)$$
$$= (1-r)(1-s)(1-t)(-1-r)(-1-s)(-1-t)$$
$$= (1^3 - 3(1^2) + 5 + 1)((-1)^3 - 5(-1)^2 + 3(-1) + 1)$$
$$= (4)(-8)$$
$$= -32$$

Therefore, $|(r^2-1)(s^2-1)(t^2-1)| = 32$.

084.

$$(r^2+1)(s^2+1)(t^2+1) = (r-i)(s-i)(t-i)(r+i)(s+i)(t+i)$$
$$= (i-r)(i-s)(i-t)(-i-r)(-i-s)(-i-t)$$
$$= (i^3 - 2i^2 + i + 1)((-i)^3 - 2(-i)^2 - i + 1)$$
$$= 3 \cdot 3$$
$$= 9$$

085.

$$\frac{1}{r} + \frac{1}{s} + \frac{1}{t} = \frac{rs + st + tr}{rst}$$
$$= \frac{-2}{-3}$$
$$= \frac{2}{3}$$

where $(x-r)(x-s)(x-t) = x^3 - (r+s+t)x^2 + (rs+st+tr)x - rst$ implies that $rs+st+tr = -2$ and $rst = -3$. Therefore, $m+n = 2+3 = 5$.

086. Before taking a reciprocal, we must get $(x+1)^3 + (x+1)^2 - 2(x+1) + 3 = 0$ where $x = r-1, s-1$, and $t-1$. Then,

$$(x+1)^3 + (x+1)^2 - 2(x+1) + 3 = x^3 + 3x^2 + 3x + 1 + x^2 + 2x + 1 - 2x - 2 + 3$$
$$= x^3 + 4x^2 + 3x + 3$$

Then, we write down the coefficients backward to get $3x^3 + 3x^2 + 4x + 1 = 0$ where the solutions are $x = \dfrac{1}{r-1}, \dfrac{1}{s-1}$ and $\dfrac{1}{t-1}$. Thus, the sum of roots in the last equation equals -1. Since we are looking at its absolute-value, we conclude that the answer is 1.

087. If we use synthetic division multiple times with -2 as its root, circle the remainders that appear until we write the division 4 times in a row (since the polynomial is in degree 4), we get $f(x-2) = x^4 - 3x^3 - 10x^2 + 43x - 37$. In fact, we can check that $f(x-2) = (x-2)^4 + 5(x-2)^3 - 4(x-2)^2 - (x-2) + 1$ equals the last expression we reached. This is another application of synthetic division, which horizontally translates the polynomial function either to the left or right. Hence, $|a| + |b| + |c| + |d| + |e| = 1 + 3 + 10 + 43 + 37 = 94$.

088. Since we know that the equation has no complex solutions, we only get real solutions. Descartes' Rule of Sign tells us that there are at most 4 positive real solutions, since the signs of coefficients of $f(x)$ alternates 4 times. On the other hand, there are at most 4 negative real roots, since the signs of coefficients of $f(-x)$ also alternates 4 times. Since the degree of the polynomial is 8, there must be 4 positive real solutions and 4 negative real solutions. Hence, the difference between the number of positive real and negative real solutions is 0.

089.

$$\sqrt{(2\sqrt{2}-3)^2} = |2\sqrt{2}-3|$$
$$= 3 - 2\sqrt{2}$$

since $\sqrt{9} = 3 > 2\sqrt{2} = \sqrt{8}$. Therefore, $A + B + C = 3 + (-2) + 2 = 3$.

090.

$$\sqrt[10]{1024} + \sqrt[9]{512} + \sqrt[8]{256} + \sqrt[7]{128} + \sqrt[6]{64} + \sqrt[5]{32} + \sqrt[4]{16} + \sqrt[3]{8} + \sqrt{4}$$
$$= 2^{10/10} + 2^{9/9} + 2^{8/8} + 2^{7/7} + 2^{6/6} + 2^{5/5} + 2^{4/4} + 2^{3/3} + 2^{2/2}$$
$$= 2 + 2 + 2 + 2 + 2 + 2 + 2 + 2 + 2$$
$$= 9(2)$$
$$= 18$$

Therefore, $n = 18$.

091.

$$\sqrt[4]{16} - \sqrt[2]{4} + \sqrt{2} = 16^{1/4} - 4^{1/2} + 2^{1/2}$$
$$= 2 - 2 + 2^{1/2}$$
$$= \sqrt{2}$$

Therefore, $n = 2$.

092.

$$\sqrt{32} - \sqrt{8} + \sqrt{2} = \sqrt{16 \cdot 2} - \sqrt{4 \cdot 2} + \sqrt{2}$$
$$= \sqrt{16}\sqrt{2} - \sqrt{4}\sqrt{2} + \sqrt{2}$$
$$= 4\sqrt{2} - 2\sqrt{2} + \sqrt{2}$$
$$= (4 - 2 + 1)\sqrt{2}$$
$$= 3\sqrt{2}$$
$$= \sqrt{9}\sqrt{2}$$
$$= \sqrt{18}$$

Therefore, $n = 18$.

093.

$$\sqrt{3 - 2\sqrt{2}} = \sqrt{A} - \sqrt{B}$$
$$3 - 2\sqrt{2} = (A + B) - 2\sqrt{AB}$$

This implies that $A + B = 3$ and $AB = 2$. Solving the system of equations, we get $(A, B) = (1, 2)$ or $(2, 1)$. Since $\sqrt{3 - 2\sqrt{2}} > 0$, we conclude that $A > B$. Thus, $A = 2$ and $B = 1$. The sum of A and B equals 3.

094.

$$\sqrt{7 - 2\sqrt{12}} = m - \sqrt{n}$$
$$7 - 2\sqrt{12} = (m^2 + n) - 2m\sqrt{n}$$
$$7 - 2\sqrt{12} = (m^2 + n) - 2\sqrt{m^2 n}$$

This implies that $m^2 + n = 7$ and $m^2 n = 12$. Thus, $(m^2, n) = (4, 3)$ or $(3, 4)$. This further implies that $(m, n) = (\pm 2, 3)$ or $(\sqrt{3}, 4)$. Since the condition stated in the problem suggests that m and n are positive integers, we conclude that $m = 2$ and $n = 3$. Hence, $m + n = 5$.

095.

$$2x^{\frac{4}{3}} + 1 = 17$$
$$2x^{\frac{4}{3}} = 16$$
$$x^{\frac{4}{3}} = 8$$
$$x = 8^{\frac{3}{4}}$$
$$x = 2^{\frac{9}{4}}$$
$$x = 2^{2\frac{1}{4}}$$
$$x = 2^2 \cdot \sqrt[4]{2}$$
$$x = 4 \cdot \sqrt[4]{2}$$

Hence, $a + b + c = 4 + 4 + 2 = 10$.

096.

$$(x-1)^{\frac{2}{3}} = 4$$
$$(x-1) = 8$$
$$x = 9$$

Hence, the value of x equals 9.

097.

$$\sqrt{x+3} - \sqrt{x-2} = 1$$
$$\sqrt{x+3} = 1 + \sqrt{x-2}$$
$$x+3 = 1 + 2\sqrt{x-2} + (x-2)$$
$$4 = 2\sqrt{x-2}$$
$$2 = \sqrt{x-2}$$
$$4 = x-2$$
$$6 = x$$

Since $x+3 > 0$ and $x-2 > 0$ at $x = 6$, this is indeed a valid solution.

098.

$$\sqrt{x+8} + \sqrt{x+1} = 7$$
$$\sqrt{x+8} = 7 - \sqrt{x+1}$$
$$x+8 = 49 - 14\sqrt{x+1} + (x+1)$$
$$-42 = -14\sqrt{x+1}$$
$$3 = \sqrt{x+1}$$
$$8 = x$$

Since $x+8 > 0$ and $x+1 > 0$ at $x = 8$, we conclude that this is valid solution.

099. Notice that the given inequality can turn into

$$\sqrt{n} > \frac{1}{61}(n - 900) + 30.$$

The graph of $y = \sqrt{x}$ passes through $(900, 30)$ and $(961, 31)$, and it is concave down, meaning that the graph of $y = \sqrt{x}$ is above the line $y = \frac{1}{61}(x - 900) + 30$ in $[900, 961]$. Hence, the number of integers satisfying the given strict inequality is 59, since $n = 901, 902, \cdots, 959$.

100. Try to look at it from the shape of the graph of $y = \sqrt[n]{x}$ where n is even. Its graph spikes up for $[0, 1]$ and slows down for $[1, \infty)$. In fact, as n becomes a large even number, its shape becomes a bit more dramatic. The graph spikes up for extremely small values of x, and then reaches 1, tending to grow infinitesimally small then-wards. Hence, $\sqrt[4000]{1,000,000} \approx 1$. You can check this result by using a calculator.

101.

$$\frac{\sqrt{a\sqrt{b\sqrt{c}}}}{\sqrt{c\sqrt{b\sqrt{a}}}} = \frac{a^{1/2}b^{1/4}c^{1/8}}{c^{1/2}b^{1/4}a^{1/8}}$$

$$= a^{3/8}b^0 c^{-3/8}$$

Hence, $|x| + |y| + |z| = \frac{6}{8} = \frac{3}{4}$. The answer is 7.

102.

$$\sqrt{2 + \sqrt{2 + \sqrt{2 + \sqrt{2 + \sqrt{\cdots}}}}} = n$$

$$2 + n = n^2$$

$$0 = n^2 - n - 2$$

$$0 = (n - 2)(n + 1)$$

$$2 = n$$

103.

$$x + 3 = \sqrt{1 - 3x}$$
$$x^2 + 6x + 9 = 1 - 3x$$
$$x^2 + 9x + 8 = 0$$
$$(x + 1)(x + 8) = 0$$

Since $x = 8$ does not hold, the only solution is $x = -1$. Hence, $|x| = 1$.

104.

$$x - 1 = \sqrt{7 - x}$$
$$x^2 - 2x + 1 = 7 - x$$
$$x^2 - x - 6 = 0$$
$$(x - 3)(x + 2) = 0$$

Since $x = -2$ does not hold, the only solution is $x = 3$. Hence, the area of the right isosceles triangle is $\frac{1}{2} \times 2 \times 2 = 2$.

105. First, compute the x-intercept by plugging $y = 0$ into the rational function to get $x = -1$. Likewise, compute the y-intercept by plugging $x = 0$ into the rational function to get $y = -2$. Hence, the product of intercepts equals 2.

106. Notice that the given function can turn into $(y - 4)(x - 1) = -4$. Hence, $(y - 4, x - 1) = (-4, 1), (4, -1), (-2, 2), (2, -2), (1, -4)$, and $(-1, 4)$. Hence, there are six possible lattice points in the graph.

On the other hand, one can solve for the values of x such that $\frac{4}{x-1}$ turns into an integer, which means that $x - 1$ is a divisor of 4. Since $x - 1$ can be either positive or negative, one can solve for

150   The Essential Workbook for Algebra 2

107.

(a)
$$y = \frac{4x-1}{x-3}$$
$$= 4 + \frac{11}{x-3}$$
$$(y-4)(x-3) = 11$$

Hence, the asymptotes are $y = 4$ and $x = 3$. The horizontal asymptote is $y = 4$. Therefore, $k = 4$.

(b)
$$y = \frac{4x^2 - 1}{x - 3}$$
$$= (4x + 12) + \frac{35}{x - 3}$$

Hence, the oblique asymptote is $y = 4x + 12$. Therefore, $m + b = 16$.

108.

$$\frac{x^2 - 1}{x - 2} = (x+2) + \frac{3}{x-2}$$
$$= (x-2) + \frac{3}{x-2} + 4$$
$$\geq 2\sqrt{(x-2)\frac{3}{x-2}} + 4$$
$$= 2\sqrt{3} + 4$$

Hence, for $x > 2$, the minimum value of y equals $4 + 2\sqrt{3}$. Hence, $a + b + c = 4 + 2 + 3 = 9$.

On the other hand, we can use quadratics to find out the bound. Let $\frac{x^2-1}{x-2} = k$ for some real k. Then, $x^2 - kx + (2k - 1) = 0$ must have some real solution x. Since $x > 2$ already indicates that x is a real value, we must look out for values of k resulting in real values of x. Thus, we know that the discriminant $(-k)^2 - 4(2k - 1) \geq 0$. This implies that, $k \geq 4 + 2\sqrt{3}$.

109.

$$y = \frac{4x^2 - 9}{2x + 3}$$
$$= \frac{(2x - 3)(2x + 3)}{2x + 3}$$
$$= 2x - 3$$

except $x = -\frac{3}{2}$. Hence, $|m + n| = |(-3) + 2| = |3 + (-2)| = 1$.

110. We perform caseworks. First, if $0 < x < 1$, then the given expression is positive. Second, if $1 < x < 2$, then the given expression is negative. Lastly, if $2 < x$, then the given expression is positive. Hence, the interval we want is $(1, 2)$. Thus, $a + b = 1 + 2 = 3$.

111.

$$\cfrac{1}{1 - \cfrac{1}{1 - \cfrac{1}{x+1}}} = \cfrac{1}{1 - \cfrac{1}{\frac{x+1}{x}}}$$
$$= \cfrac{1}{1 - 1 - \cfrac{1}{x}}$$
$$= -x$$
$$= -100$$

Hence, $x = 100$.

112.

$$\cfrac{1}{2 - \cfrac{2}{2 - \cfrac{2}{x+2}}} = \cfrac{1}{2 - \cfrac{2}{\frac{x+2}{x+1}}}$$
$$= \cfrac{1}{\frac{2x + 2 - x - 2}{x + 1}}$$
$$= \frac{x + 1}{x}$$
$$= 2$$

Therefore, $x + 1 = 2x$ implies that $x = 1$.

113.

(a)

$$2^{3(x-1)} \leq 2^6$$
$$3x - 3 \leq 6$$
$$3x \leq 9$$
$$x \leq 3$$

Hence, the maximum possible value of x equals 3.

(b)

$$\left(\frac{1}{3}\right)^{1-3x} \leq 3^5$$
$$3^{3x-1} \leq 3^5$$
$$3x - 1 \leq 5$$
$$3x \leq 6$$
$$x \leq 2$$

Hence, the maximum possible value of x equals 2.

(c)

$$\left(\frac{2}{7}\right)^x \leq \left(\frac{7}{2}\right)^{6-3x}$$
$$\left(\frac{7}{2}\right)^{-x} \leq \left(\frac{7}{2}\right)^{6-3x}$$
$$-x \leq 6 - 3x$$
$$2x \leq 6$$
$$x \leq 3$$

Hence, the maximum possible value of x equals 3.

114.

$$9^x - 12 \cdot 3^x + 27 = 0$$
$$(3^x)^2 - 12 \cdot 3^x + 27 = 0$$
$$(3^x - 9)(3^x - 3) = 0$$
$$3^x = 9, 3$$

Hence, $x = 2$ or 1. The sum of roots must be 3.

115.

$$8 \cdot \left(\frac{1}{2}\right)^{2x} + 2 \cdot \left(\frac{1}{2}\right)^x - 1 = 0$$
$$(4(\frac{1}{2})^x - 1)(2(\frac{1}{2})^x + 1) = 0$$

Hence, $(\frac{1}{2})^x = \frac{1}{4}$ implies $x = 2$. It is easy to check that $(\frac{1}{2})^x > 0$ so $(\frac{1}{2})^x = -\frac{1}{2}$ has no real solution.

116. Continuously compound interest rate model can be written as $P_0 e^{rt}$ where P_0 is the initial population, r is the annual interest rate, and t is the number of years passed since the initial state. Hence,

$$2000 e^{0.04(100)} = 2000 e^4$$

Thus, $a = 2000$ and $b = 4$. Thus, the sum of a and b equals 2004.

117.

(a)

$$\log_4 16 = k$$
$$4^k = 16$$
$$k = 2$$

(b)

$$\log_3 243 = k$$
$$3^k = 243$$
$$k = 5$$

(c)

$$\log_{17} 289 = k$$
$$17^k = 289$$
$$k = 2$$

118.

$$3 = \log_{10}(1000) \leq \log_{10}(1005) < \log_{10}(1050) < \log_{10}(1500) < \log_{10}(10000) = 4$$

implies that all three logarithmic expressions are close to 3 with its decimal expression negligible. The reasoning behind this is that 1005, 1050, and 1500 is way much closer to 1000 than to 10000. Hence, the sum of these numbers can be approximated to 9.

In fact, we can approximate the value of $\log_{10}(1005)$ by a linear function $y = \frac{1}{9000}(x - 1000) + 3$. If we substitute $x = 1005$ into the linear equation, $y = 3\frac{1}{1800}$, which is an underestimate of the actual value, $3.002166\cdots$. Likewise, we can substitute $x = 1050$ and $x = 1500$ to find out that the estimate values are extremely close to 3. Hence, adding these three values results in a value closer to 9 than to 10.

119.

(a)

$$\log(x) + \log(x - 7) = \log(30)$$
$$\log(x(x - 7)) = \log(30)$$
$$x(x - 7) = 30$$
$$x = 10, -3$$

Since $x > 0$ and $x - 7 > 0$, we conclude that $x = -3$ is extraneous. Hence, $x = 10$ is the only real solution.

(b)

$$\log(x - 5) - \log(x - 3) = \log\left(\frac{1}{3}\right)$$
$$\log\left(\frac{x - 5}{x - 3}\right) = \log\left(\frac{1}{3}\right)$$
$$\frac{x - 5}{x - 3} = \frac{1}{3}$$
$$3x - 15 = x - 3$$
$$2x = 12$$
$$x = 6$$

Since $x - 5 > 0$ and $x - 3 > 0$ at $x = 6$, this is a valid solution.

120.

(a)
$$\begin{aligned}\log_4(2^4) + \log_2(2^3) &= \log_4(16) + 3\log_2(2) \\ &= \log_4(4^2) + 3\log_2(2) \\ &= 2\log_4(4) + 3\log_2(2) \\ &= 2 + 3 \\ &= 5\end{aligned}$$

(b)
$$\begin{aligned}\log_3(243) - \log_3(9) &= \log_3(3^5) - \log_3(3^2) \\ &= 5\log_3(3) - 2\log_3(3) \\ &= 5 - 2 \\ &= 3\end{aligned}$$

(c)
$$\begin{aligned}\log_7\left(\frac{1}{49}\right) + \log_7(343) &= \log_7(7^{-2}) + \log_7(7^3) \\ &= -2\log_7(7) + 3\log_7(7) \\ &= -2 + 3 \\ &= 1\end{aligned}$$

(d)
$$\begin{aligned}\log_5(125) + \log_5(625) &= \log_5(5^3) + \log_5(5^4) \\ &= 3\log_5(5) + 4\log_5(5) \\ &= 3 + 4 \\ &= 7\end{aligned}$$

121. Let $t = \log_3(x)$. Then, $t^2 + 2t - 3 = (t+3)(t-1) = 0$ implies that $\log_3(x) = -3$ or $\log_3(x) = 1$. Hence, $x = 3^{-3}$ or $x = 3^1$. Thus, $x = \dfrac{1}{27}$ and $x = 3$. Therefore, the sum of solutions must be $\dfrac{82}{27}$, so the answer is $m + n = 82 + 27 = 109$.

122.

$$9^x + 6^x - 2 \cdot 4^x = 0$$
$$\left(\dfrac{3^x}{2^x}\right)^2 + \left(\dfrac{3}{2}\right)^x - 2 = 0$$
$$\left(\left(\dfrac{3}{2}\right)^x + 2\right)\left(\left(\dfrac{3}{2}\right)^x - 1\right) = 0$$
$$\left(\dfrac{3}{2}\right)^x = 1$$
$$x = 0$$

123. Let a_n be the number of seats in the nth row. Then, $a_n = 15 + 3(n-1) = 12 + 3n$. Hence, at the last row, there are $a_{35} = 12 + 3(35) = 117$ number of seats.

124. Let a_n be the value of nth term in the arithmetic sequence. Then, $a_n = 100 - 3(n-1) = 103 - 3n$. Hence, $a_{10} = 103 - 3(10) = 73$.

125.
(a) The arithmetic mean of 5 and 9 can be found by $\dfrac{5+9}{2} = 7$.

(b) The arithmetic mean of 101, 102, $\cdots$, 108, can be found by the average of 1, 2, $\cdots$, 8, added by 100. Hence, the answer is 104.5.

126. The arithmetic mean of the first 101 positive integers equals
$$\dfrac{1+2+3+\cdots+101}{101} = \dfrac{\dfrac{101(1+101)}{2}}{101} = \dfrac{102}{2} = 51.$$

127. Let b_n be the nth term of a geometric sequence. Then, $b_n = 2 \cdot 2^{n-1}$. Hence, $b_8 = 2 \cdot 2^7 = 2^8 = 256$.

128. Let b_n be the nth term of a geometric sequence. Then, $b_n = 2\left(\sqrt{2}\right)^{n-1}$. Hence, $b_5 = 2\left(\sqrt{2}\right)^4 = 2 \cdot 4 = 8$.

On the other hand, let $f(x) = a(\sqrt{2})^x$ where $f(1) = \sqrt{2}$. Hence, $a = \sqrt{2}$. Since the fifth term equals $f(5)$, we plug $x = 5$ into the function to find out $f(5) = \sqrt{5}(\sqrt{5})^5 = 8$.

129. First, the arithmetic mean of 4 and 16 equals $\dfrac{4+16}{2} = 10$. On the other hand, the geometric mean of 4 and 16 equals $\sqrt{4 \times 16} = 8$. Hence, the difference between the two values equals 2.

130. For positive real x, AM-GM inequality states that

$$\frac{x^2 + \dfrac{1}{x^2}}{2} \geq \sqrt{x^2 \cdot \dfrac{1}{x^2}}$$

where the equality holds if $x^2 = \dfrac{1}{x^2}$. Now, the minimum value must be 2 at $x^4 = 1$, which implies that $x = 1$. The value of n equals 2.

131.

(a)

$$\begin{aligned} S_{10} &= \frac{10(a_1 + a_{10})}{2} \\ &= 5(a_1 + a_{10}) \\ &= 5(5 + 41) \\ &= 230 \end{aligned}$$

(b)

$$\begin{aligned} S_7 &= \frac{7(a_1 + a_7)}{2} \\ &= \frac{7(2 + 20)}{2} \\ &= 77 \end{aligned}$$

132.

(a)
$$S_5 = \frac{2\left(1-\left(\frac{1}{2}\right)^5\right)}{1-\frac{1}{2}}$$
$$= 4\left(1-\frac{1}{32}\right)$$
$$= \frac{31}{8}$$

Hence, $\frac{m}{n} = \frac{31}{8}$, so $m+n = 31+8 = 39$.

(b)
$$S = \frac{4}{1-\left(-\frac{1}{2}\right)}$$
$$= \frac{4}{\frac{3}{2}}$$
$$= \frac{8}{3}$$

Hence, $\frac{m}{n} = \frac{8}{3}$, so $m+n = 11$.

133.

$$\sum_{k=1}^{20}(k+1)(k+2) = \sum_{k=1}^{20}(k^2+3k+2)$$
$$= \left(\frac{20 \cdot 21 \cdot 41}{6}\right) + 3\left(\frac{20 \cdot 21}{2}\right) + 2 \cdot 20$$
$$= 70 \cdot 41 + 30 \cdot 21 + 40$$
$$= 2870 + 630 + 40$$
$$= 3540$$

134.

$$\sum_{k=1}^{7}(k+1)^3 = \sum_{l=2}^{8} l^3$$
$$= 2^3 + 3^3 + 4^3 + \cdots + 8^3$$
$$= (1^3 + 2^3 + \cdots + 8^3) - (1^3)$$
$$= \left(\frac{8(1+8)}{2}\right)^2 - 1$$
$$= 1296 - 1$$
$$= 1295$$

135.

$$S = \frac{1}{2} + \frac{2}{2^2} + \frac{3}{2^3} + \cdots$$
$$\frac{1}{2}S = \frac{1}{2^2} + \frac{2}{2^3} + \frac{3}{2^4} + \cdots$$
$$\left(1 - \frac{1}{2}\right)S = \frac{1}{2} + \frac{1}{2^2} + \frac{1}{2^3} + \cdots$$
$$\frac{1}{2}S = \frac{1/2}{1 - 1/2}$$
$$S = 2$$

136. Since $S_n = a_1 + a_2 + \cdots + a_{n-1} + a_n$ and $S_{n-1} = a_1 + a_2 + \cdots + a_{n-1}$, we get $a_n = S_n - S_{n-1}$. Hence,

$$a_{10} = S_{10} - S_9$$
$$= (4(10)^2 + 3(10) + 1) - (4(9)^2 + 3(9) + 1)$$
$$= 431 - 352$$
$$= 79$$

137. Compute the consecutive differences as 6, 10, 14, and 18. The consecutive differences of the previous consecutive differences equal 4, 4, and 4. Since there are two layers of differences until we reach the layer of constant differences, we conclude that $k = 2$. Since $y = x^2$ has the standard difference of 2! in its last difference layer, we conclude that $a_k = a_2 = 2$. Hence, the product of a_k and k equals 4.

138. Compute the consecutive differences as 9, 23, 43, 69, and 101. Now, the consecutive differences of the previous consecutive differences equal 14, 20, 26 and 32. Finally, compute the consecutive differences of this second layer of differences as 6, 6, and 6. Since there are three layers of differences until we reach the layer of constant differences, we conclude that $k = 3$. Since $y = x^3$ has the standard difference of 3! in its last difference layer, we conclude that $a_k = a_3 = 1$. Hence, the sum of a_k and k equals 4.

139. This is a typical Fibonacci sequence, $F_n = F_{n-1} + F_{n-2}$ where F_n counts the number of ways Bob can walk n-steps using 1-step or 2-steps only.

$$F_1 = 1$$
$$F_2 = 2$$
$$F_3 = 3$$
$$F_4 = 5$$
$$F_5 = 8$$
$$F_6 = 13$$
$$F_7 = 21$$
$$F_8 = 34$$
$$F_9 = 55$$
$$F_{10} = 89$$

140. Let a_n be the number of n-steps ending with 1-step and b_n be the number of n-steps ending with 2-steps. Then, it is easy to check that $a_n = a_{n-1} + b_{n-1}$ and $b_n = a_{n-2}$, according to the given condition. Hence,

k	1	2	3	4	5	6	7	8	9	10
a_k	1	1	2	3	4	6	9	13	19	28
b_k	0	1	1	1	2	3	4	6	9	13

Hence, $a_{10} + b_{10} = 41$.

141. We perform caseworks.

- $x + y = 3$ implies $(x, y) = (1, 2), (2, 1)$.
- $x + y = 6$ implies $(x, y) = (1, 5), (2, 4), (3, 3), (4, 2)$, and $(5, 1)$.
- $x + y = 9$ implies $(x, y) = (3, 6), 94, 5), (5, 4), (6, 3)$.
- $x + y = 12$ implies $(x, y) = (6, 6)$.

Hence, there are 12 cases.

142. We use Legendre function and the principle of inclusion and exclusion to find out the number of multiples of 5 or 7 for integers ranging from 1 to 100. In other words,

$$\lfloor \frac{100}{5} \rfloor + \lfloor \frac{100}{7} \rfloor - \lfloor \frac{100}{35} \rfloor = 20 + 14 - 2 = 32$$

143. Since there are two choices for x_is, three choices for y_is and four choices for z_is, we compute it as $2 \times 3 \times 4 = 24$.

144. This directly uses the definition of multiplication in counting. We simply take a product of 4 and 5, since counts are progressively ongoing. Hence, the answer must be 20.

145. This uses the definition of permutation. In other words, the top 8 positions will be filled by

$$16 \times 15 \times 14 \times 13 \times 12 \times 11 \times 10 \times 9 = \binom{16}{8} \times 8! = 2^8 \cdot 3^4 \cdot 5^2 \cdot 7^1 \cdot 11^1 \cdot 13^1$$

Hence, $f(n) = (8+1)(4+1)(2+1)(1+1)(1+1)(1+1) = 1080$.

146.

(a) $\binom{6}{3} = \frac{6 \times 5 \times 4}{3 \times 2 \times 1} = 20$.

(b) $\binom{6}{4} = \frac{6 \times 5 \times 4 \times 3}{4 \times 3 \times 2 \times 1} = 15$.

147. First, categorize the set of numbers into $\{1, 8\}, \{2, 7\}, \{3, 6\}, \{4, 5\}$. It is easy to notice that if 1 is chosen, for example, then 8 cannot be selected. Likewise, we must select one number from each category to satisfy the given condition. Hence, choose one from each category and arrange them in a row in $2^4 \times 4! = 384$ number of ways.

148. There could be one common club or none. First, assume there is no common club. Then, there are 6 possible cases for Alice and Bob to join two clubs each. In particular, (Alice, Bob) = (12, 34), (13, 24), (14, 23), (23, 14), (24, 13), (34, 12), where 1, 2, 3, and 4 refers to the four clubs they must join. On the other hand, if we assume there is one common club, then there are 24 possible cases for Alice and Bob to join. First, choose the common club they must join. For each common club, there are $3 \times 2 = 6$ number of ways for Alice and Bob to choose different clubs. Hence, there are $4 \times 6 = 24$ number of ways for them to join clubs, having one common club. That being written, we add up 6 and 24 to conclude that there are 30 total cases for them to join the clubs.

149. First, choosing three evens and two odds results in $\binom{4}{3} \times \binom{4}{2} = 4 \times 6 = 24$ number of ways. Second, choosing one even and four odds results in $\binom{4}{1} \times \binom{4}{4} = 4$ number of ways. Hence, there are 28 number of ways that the sum of all face values of 5 cards is even.

150. Since novels and comic books are not necessarily non-adjacent, we compute the number of arrangements of these books by $7! = 7 \times 6 \times 5 \times 4 \times 3 \times 2 \times 1$ ways. Now, since history books must be non-adjacent, we find out there are 8 spots for the first history book to be placed. Then, there are 7 spots for the second history book to be placed afterwards. Hence, there are $8 \times 7 \times 7! = 282240$ number of arrangements satisfying the given condition.

151. First, place all comic books into a single bundle, which results in five-letter arrangements. However, we can arrange the comic books inside the bundle, so there are

$$5! \times 3! = 120 \times 6 = 720$$

number of arrangements of all these books, satisfying the given condition.

152. This is a typical circular permutation problem. Circular permutation always gets rid of over-counts that naturally arise when configuration is rotated. In fact, one configuration is considered equal to another configuration if one can be rotated to match with another one. First, we assume all six spots are distinct, so we arrange six people in 6! ways. However, since (1, 2, 3, 4, 5, 6), (2, 3, 4, 5, 6, 1), (3, 4, 5, 6, 1, 2), (4, 5, 6, 1, 2, 3), (5, 6, 1, 2, 3, 4), and (6, 1, 2, 3, 4, 5) are considered equal, we divide 6! by 6. Hence, there are $5! (= 120)$ number of arrangements of six people around a circular table.

153. Let Bob be seated. Then, Bo can be seated in two possible seats. Let all the others be seated. Hence, there are $2 \times 5! = 240$ number of ways for all seven people to be seated around the circular table.

154. Let Alice be seated. Then, Bob can be seated in three possible seats. Let all the others be seated. Hence, there are $3 \times 4! = 72$ number of ways for all six people to be seated around the circular table.

155. Let's use the multiplication principle of probability. Probability of selecting "distinct" kinds must take order into account. In other words, the probability we want equals

$$\left(\frac{3}{5} \times \frac{2}{5} \times \frac{2}{5}\right) \times 3 = \frac{36}{125}$$

Hence, $m + n = 36 + 125 = 161$.

156. This is a typical conditional probability. First, the sample space never equals the set of all primes. In fact, the new sample space we deal with is $\{2, 3, 5, 7, 11, 13, 17\}$. Hence, we are looking at the proportion(=probability) of primes smaller than 10, out of primes smaller than 18. Hence, the probability we look for equals

$$\frac{|\{2, 3, 5, 7\}|}{|\{2, 3, 5, 7, 11, 13, 17\}|} = \frac{4}{7}$$

Hence, $m + n = 4 + 7 = 11$.

157.
Solution 1 We use direct casework.

$$\frac{1}{3} \times \frac{3}{4} + \frac{2}{3} \times \frac{1}{4} = \frac{5}{12}$$

Solution 2 We use the principle of inclusion and exclusion.

$$\left(\frac{1}{3} + \frac{1}{4} - \frac{1}{3} \cdot \frac{1}{4}\right) - \left(\frac{1}{3} \cdot \frac{1}{4}\right) = \frac{5}{12}$$

Hence, the answer equals $m + n = 5 + 12 = 17$.

158.

Solution 1 We use combinations to solve the problem.
$$\frac{\binom{3}{1} \cdot \binom{4}{1}}{\binom{7}{2}} = \frac{4}{7}$$

Solution 2 We use the multiplication principle of probability.
$$\left(\frac{3}{7} \times \frac{4}{6}\right) \times 2! = \frac{4}{7}$$

Hence, the answer equals $m + n = 4 + 7 = 11$.

159. Since the nickels are "indistinguishable" kinds, we do NOT multiply by the number of arrangements in the end as we do it for "distinct" kinds. In other words,
$$p = \frac{3}{11} \times \frac{2}{10} = \frac{3}{55}$$

Hence, $m + n = 3 + 55 = 58$.

160. Since two blue marbles are taken out, the sample space consists of five blue and six red marbles. It is easy to use complementary probability to compute p, which equals
$$1 - \left(\frac{5}{11} \times \frac{4}{10}\right) = \frac{9}{11}$$

Hence, $m + n = 9 + 11 = 20$.

161. We use the principle of inclusion and exclusion to compute p, which equals
$$\frac{3 + 2 - 1}{6} = \frac{4}{6} = \frac{2}{3}$$

Hence, $m + n = 2 + 3 = 5$.

162. Since the order has been already set, we don't need to worry about multiplying by the number of arrangements in the end. In particular,,
$$p = \frac{3}{4} \times \frac{3}{4} \times \frac{3}{4} \times \frac{1}{4} = \frac{27}{256}$$

Hence, $m + n = 27 + 256 = 283$.

163. The sample space consists of 15 events, since the given condition states that there is at least one head. We only need to count the number of events with two heads, i.e.,
$$p = \frac{\binom{4}{2}}{15} = \frac{6}{15} = \frac{2}{5}$$

Hence, $m + n = 2 + 5 = 7$.

164. Using combinations to compute the probability, we get

$$\frac{\binom{6}{3} \times \binom{9}{2}}{\binom{15}{5}} = \frac{240}{7 \times 11 \times 13}$$

Hence, the sum of distinct prime factors of n equals $7 + 11 + 13 = 31$.

165. According to the definition of expected value, we get

$$E(X) = 1 \cdot \frac{1}{4} + 2 \cdot \frac{1}{3} + 3 \cdot \frac{1}{4} + 4 \cdot \frac{1}{6} = \frac{7}{3}$$

Hence, $m + n = 10$.

166. According to the variance formula, $Var(X) = E(X^2) - (E(X))^2$, we get

$$Var(X) = \left(1^2 \cdot \frac{1}{4} + 2^2 \cdot \frac{1}{4} + 3^2 \cdot \frac{1}{4} + 4^2 \cdot \frac{1}{4}\right) - 6.25$$
$$= \frac{1 + 4 + 9 + 16}{4} - \frac{25}{4}$$
$$= \frac{30}{4} - \frac{25}{4}$$
$$= \frac{5}{4}$$
$$= 1.25$$

167. According to the binomial distribution model, we easily get

$$p = \binom{5}{3} \times \left(\frac{1}{5}\right)^3 \times \left(\frac{4}{5}\right)^2 = \frac{32}{625}$$

Hence, $m + n = 32 + 625 = 657$.

168. The standard normal distribution uses $Z = \dfrac{X - \mu}{\sigma}$ to transform the normal distribution into the standard one. Hence,

$$Z = \frac{3 - 0.5}{2} = \frac{2.5}{2} = \frac{5}{4}$$

where $m + n = 5 + 4 = 9$.

169. The actual mean is likely to be in the interval $[20 - 2, 20 + 2]$ or $(20 - 2, 20 + 2)$. Hence, $(A, B) = (18, 22)$. Thus, $A + B = 40$.

170. Since the samples are randomly selected from the same population, the margin of error can only be decreased by the sample size. Since Y has a smaller margin of error, it means it has larger sample. This indicates that the actual mean is more likely to be in Y than in X. Hence, the answer is 200.

The Essential Workbook for
Algebra 2

초판발행   2024년 3월 29일

저자　　유하림
발행인　최영민
발행처　헤르몬하우스
주소　　경기도 파주시 신촌로 16
전화　　031-8071-0088
팩스　　031-942-8688
전자우편　hermonh@naver.com
출판등록　2015년 3월 27일
등록번호　제406-2015-31호

ⓒ 유하림 2024, Printed in Korea.

ISBN 979-11-92520-87-2 (53410)

- 정가는 뒤표지에 있습니다.
- 헤르몬하우스는 피앤피북의 임프린트 출판사입니다.
- 이 책의 어느 부분도 저작권자나 발행인의 승인 없이 무단 복제하여 이용힐 수 없습니다.
- 파본 및 낙장은 구입하신 서점에서 교환하여 드립니다.